Backyard Pioneers
Fortbuilders

   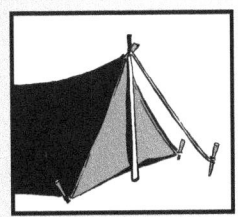 

Story Quest Walks

BY

MENTOR AGILITY

Copyright 2024 Mentor Agility LLC
Mentor Agility LLC
Jackson Hole, WY 83001
MentorAgility.com

ISBN: 979-8-9853539-7-6

Designed & Illustrated by Kevin Gleason

Backyard Pioneers: Fort Builders

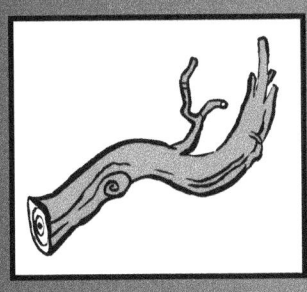
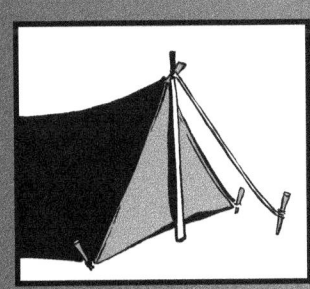

activity menu

story and imagination

architect's model

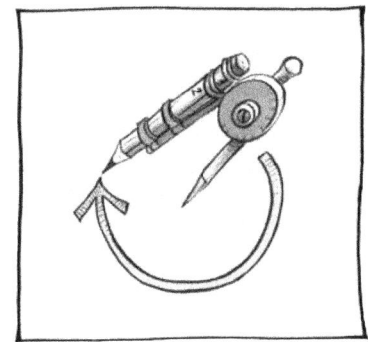

construction

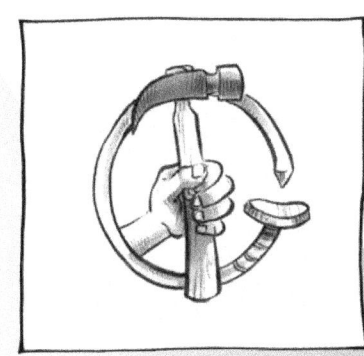

fortbuiler's journal

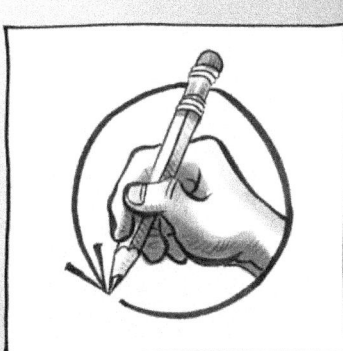

1

Box
Forts

Box Forts

Fort Focus: Before you recycle your cardboard boxes, why not make a fort or two? This activity will show you how to create simple, yet fun forts from boxes that can be revised or re-created anytime you choose.

Structure Story: Can you imagine living in a world that didn't have cardboard boxes? It's difficult! Do a survey of cardboard boxes in your house, garage and storage areas. Make tally marks under the right category for each box you find.

Small Boxes	Medium-sized Boxes	Large Boxes
(shoe box or smaller)	(shoe box to apple crate)	(larger than an apple crate)

Boxes are everywhere. The first box was produced in England in 1817, and the first box made in the United States was in 1895. For almost two hundred years there have been boxes for manufacturers to ship their products, for parents to wrap gifts and for children to use to make forts!

Try this: Add some design elements to the box on the next page to create some unique ideas for a fort.

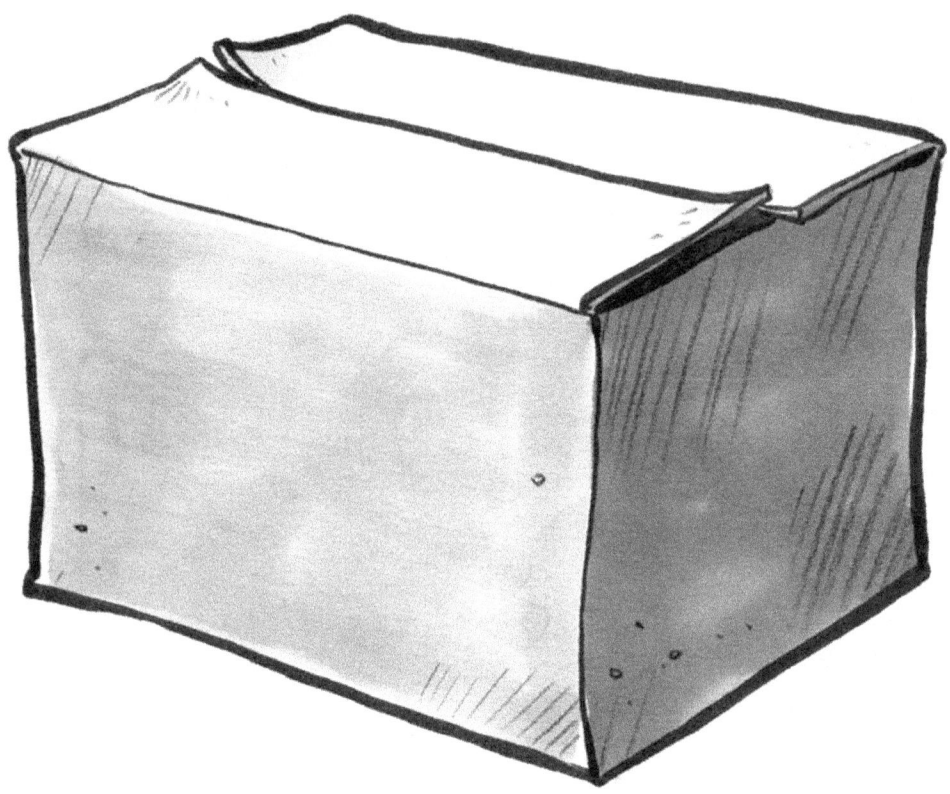

One rainy day, two friends sat wondering what to do. The electricity had gone out, so there was no television to watch and no video games to play. It seemed like there was no way to have fun.

One of the friend's mother said, "Why don't you two go into the garage. There might just be something fun to do in there."

Slowly the two ambled into the cold, dirty garage. They looked around, fiddled with some cans they found, and then they spied the stack of empty boxes. When the electricity finally came on the mother called them in.

"Do we have to come in? We're having so much fun with these boxes!" said one of the kids.

A Story Activity: In the space on the next page, illustrate or write about what the two kids in the story above did with the boxes they found in the garage.
We all know how much fun boxes can be. After you finish the story activity, try building some box forts!

Fortbuilders

architect's model

Activity Blueprint

Fort Journal: Keep a record of your fort building experiences on the Fort Journal pages at the end of this chapter. On the journal pages, you can make notes, draw sketches, and attach photographs of your fort building experience.

A Model Idea: Build your models on a base made of cardboard.

Box Model: A Box City

Materials

- 24" x 24" or larger piece of cardboard for the base
- An assortment of small boxes, such as butter boxes, cereal boxes, candy boxes, and others
- White glue
- Low–temperature glue gun and glue sticks
- Construction paper
- Colored markers
- Tools: scissors

Step 1: Create buildings out of boxes.

Decide what kinds of buildings your box city needs.

Make buildings by covering boxes with construction paper, gluing the paper in place and decorating the outside with windows, doors, and other elements.

Make as many buildings as your imagination and a pile of small boxes will allow.

Step 2: Plan your box city.

Lay out the cardboard base.

Decide where the different buildings will go and where you will need roads, parks and other details that are not made with boxes.

Before you attach the boxes with glue, make light pencil marks on the base to show where to place each box.

Step 3: Build your box city.

Glue the buildings in place.

Use markers to create roads and other flat features.

Make trees and other three-dimensional items out of construction paper or leftover boxes.

Step 4: Play with your model.

Get some toy vehicles, people, and animals, and use your imagination to have a box of fun!

 construction

A Child-Sized Fort

There are two simple box forts outlined here. One is a Stacked Box Fort and the other is an Oversized Box Fort. Cut them, decorate them, and play with them. When you have finished, be sure to recycle them!

Parent Tip: Building with boxes is fun, inexpensive and easy. You may need to help your child with box cutting, since box knives or utility knives can be extremely dangerous if used improperly.

Box Fort #1:

Stacked Box Fort

Materials

- A large assortment of medium-sized cardboard boxes approximately the size of a standard apple crate
- A large sheet of flat cardboard or a light blanket or tarp for the roof
- Markers
- Masking tape 3/4" wide or wider
- Tools: scissors, utility knife. *See Parent Tip above.*

Step 1: Assess the box collection.
Do you have enough boxes? If not, where could you get more?
Sort boxes according to size and structural condition.

Step 2: Find a location for your fort.
Get permission to build your box fort in a place that is safe, relatively flat, and out of the way so that you won't have to take it down too soon.
Prepare the building site by removing unwanted items that are in the way.

Step 3: Experiment with the boxes.
Start stacking boxes to see what kind of fort you can create.

As you build a second or third row, be sure to stagger the boxes so that joints do not line-up as shown in the second illustration below:

Yes!   No!

Step 4: Decorate the fort.
Use markers, paper and whatever else you can think of to decorate your fort.
Get help to cut holes or remove box parts.

Step 5: Build a roof.
If you want a roof on your fort, use a blanket, tarp or large piece of flat cardboard.
Caution: Do not stand on the boxes or the roof.

Step 6: Play in your stacked box fort.

Box Fort #2:

Oversized Box Fort

Materials

- One or more large appliance boxes
- Markers
- Masking tape 3/4" wide or wider
- Latex paint
- Scrap rolls and sheets of paper
- Low-temperature glue gun and glue sticks
- Tools: utility knife, scissors, paintbrushes, paint shirts
- See Parent Tip above.

Step 1: Find the perfect place for your fort.
Oversized box forts can take a lot of space, so find a location for your fort that offers what you need.

Clear away debris and other obstacles so that you have plenty of work and play space.

Step 2: Experiment with your boxes.
Place the boxes in different ways to help you decide just how you want to build your fort.
Get more boxes if you do not have enough.

Step 3: Make adjustments to your box.
Get help cutting windows, doors, box tops or bottoms, and other things you need to cut.
Use tape to connect boxes or to make repairs. Get permission before taping anything to walls.

Step 4: Decorate the fort.
Now comes the fun. Use markers, paint, paper, and whatever your imagination and parents allow.

Step 5: Play with the fort.
Oversized box forts are really versatile. For a while they might be frontier forts. Later they could become space forts or an underwater fort.

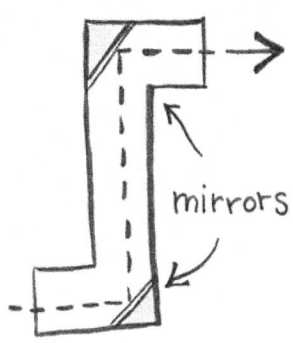

mirrors

A cardboard periscope!

Using two mirrors , some tape, and extra box cardboard, you can create a periscope to help you see over walls and around corners.

Box Forts

Fort Construction Dates:

My Plan: Make a building plan. Take photos of the site before you build, the people who are helping you, and activities such as gathering materials. Put the photos here.

Construction: Tell about what happened as you built. Did things go as planned? What was fun? What was difficult? Add more photos and sketches.

After Building: How have you used your new fort? What kinds of fun have you had? Write, draw, add photos and record the pleasures of having a fort!

Media Connection: Make a media journal to go along with your writing and sketches. Take photographs and create a photomontage or Keynote presentation. Record your fort building on video, and make a film of your experience using Final Cut Pro or Final Cut Express.

Post your media project on the Apple Student Gallery.

Review tutorials for Keynote, Final Cut Pro, and Final Cut Express. Tutorials can be found at www. apple.com. Select support and then the program that you are using.

2

Sawhorse
Forts

Sawhorse Forts

Fort Focus: Forts come in all shapes and sizes. Some are complex, some are simple and some are adaptable. Sawhorse forts are both simple and adaptable. They can go up in minutes, be moved easily and be changed to fit new locations and needs.

Structure Story:

*T*he twins lived in an apartment building with a small yard. One day they decided to build a fort. Unfortunately, they couldn't decide whether it would be a stopping place for traveling royalty or a hiding place for military maneuvers. At first the disagreement was mild, but the longer the two talked the more determined each became.

Creative Thinking: If you could build any fort that you wanted to, what would it be like? Draw or describe it to the right:

The twins' dad, who was cleaning up the morning's dishes, suggested that if they went outside for a while, a solution might come to them as they played.

*As they rode their bikes past a building site right up the street, a loud **THUMP** surprised them! After bringing their bikes to a stop, they both looked at the workers. The sound had been made when one worker dropped a piece of plywood on two sawhorses. Almost simultaneously the twins said, "We could make a sawhorse fort!"*

They quickly turned their bikes towards home, chattering all the way.

"You could make one side into your royalty fort and…"

"And you could make your army fort on the other."

They knew their Dad had a set of sawhorses in the garage. Now all they needed to do was to get his permission to use them, find some plywood and build some forts!

A Story Activity: Think about the forts the twins want to make. Make a list of all the other kinds of sawhorse forts they could construct.

architect's model

Activity Blueprint

Fort Journal: Keep a record of your fort building experiences on the Fort Journal pages at the end of this activity. On the journal pages, you can make notes, draw sketches, and attach photographs of your fort building experience.

A Model Idea: Build your models on a base of plywood or sheathing material.

Sawhorse Fort Experiments

Materials
• Plywood or sheathing material 1/2" or thicker, 24" x 24" or larger
• Popsicle sticks
• Small pieces of thin wood to fit on sawhorses
• Colored construction paper or strips of plastic
• White glue
• Tools: Low-temperature glue gun and glue sticks

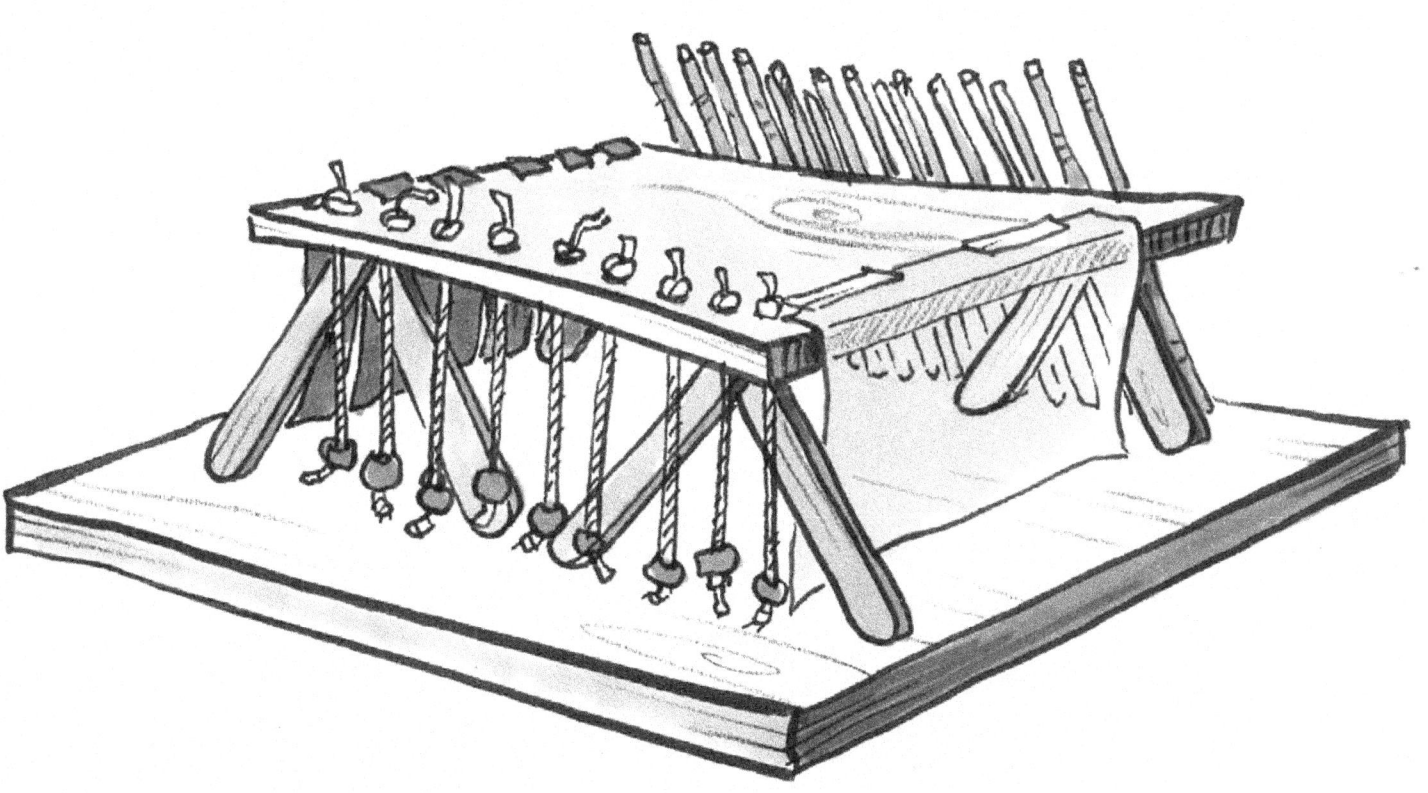

Directions: Follow the steps below to help you experiment with all kinds of forts that could be made from sawhorses. Use your imagination! This will help you decide which fort you want to make.

Step 1: Make some model sawhorses.

❧ Take two Popsicle sticks and create one end of a sawhorse by gluing the two together where the tops slightly overlap as shown to the right. Each sawhorse requires two of these ends. Make as many as you will need for the number of models you want to make.

❧ When you have two sawhorse ends, glue a Popsicle stick across the top of two ends to create a sawhorse that is freestanding. Repeat the process until you have the number of sawhorses you need for your model.

Step 2: Make the sawhorse fort.

❧ Set two sawhorses parallel to one another.

❧ Place a small piece of wood across the tops of the two sawhorses to create the fort's roof.

❧ Create solid fort sides by cutting strips of paper and attaching them to the roof with glue. Decorate the fort sides before gluing to the wood. Create imaginative or camouflaged sides by cutting narrow strips of paper or plastic, decorating the strips, and attaching the strips to the roof.

❧ Your choice of paper or plastic colors or patterns will help you make the fort become what you want it to be.

Step 3: Play with the model!

A Child-Sized Fort

Are you ready to make a sawhorse fort? Do you know what it will look like when it is finished, or are you going to let it evolve? Where are you going to put it? Read the simple steps below to help you make a quick and fun sawhorse fort!

Parent Tip: Sawhorses come in many styles and conditions. Some are pre-made, some require some assembly, some are heavy duty and some are much are lighter. Help your child choose a set that will serve her needs for the best price as well as usability.

Materials
• Two sawhorses of the same size for each fort
• Roof material: plywood, sheathing or tarp
• White glue
• Large sheets of paper, poster board, cardboard, etc.
• Pushpins or staples
• Tools: Scissors, low-temperature glue gun and glue sticks, staple gun

Directions:

Step 1: Locate the fort.

❧ Find a relatively level fort location. Be sure to get permission for your fort's placement. Sawhorse forts work well indoors and outdoors. Remove any obstructions from your fort area.

Step 2: Assemble the sawhorse fort structure.

❧ Place two sawhorses parallel to one another so that the roof material will fit safely. There is no need to overlap too much on the sawhorse ends.

❧ *Caution! Do not climb on the roof of your fort.*

❧ Place roof plywood or sheathing on the sawhorses. If you are using a tarp for a roof, secure it to the sawhorse with pushpins or staples.

Step 3: Construct the sawhorse fort walls.

- Use cardboard, poster board, large pieces of paper or paper strips to create the fort walls. Decorate side panels before attaching to the roof. Glue, staple or use pushpins to connect the side pieces to your fort roof.

Step 4: Use your fort.

- If you built your fort outside, you will need to secure the bottom of the walls so that the wind doesn't disturb them.

- Use your imagination to play in your fort and change it when you have new ideas.

- Build another fort, and travel between the two. Possibly, build one fort at each neighborhood friend's house, and design games and activities that take you from place to place!

 *fortbuilder's journal*

Sawhorse Fort

Construction Dates:

My Plan: Make a building plan. Take photos of the site before you build, of gathering materials, of the people who will be helping and add them here. (You can use the space to the left as well.)

Construction: Tell about what happened as you built. Did things go as planned? What was fun? What was hard? Add more photos and sketches.

After Building: How have you used your new fort? What kinds of fun have you had? Write, draw, add photos and record the pleasures of having a fort!

Media Connection: Make a media journal to go along with your writing and sketches. Take photographs and create a photomontage or Keynote presentation. Record your fort building on video, and make a film of your experience using Final Cut Pro or Final Cut Express.

Post your media project on the Apple Student Gallery.

Review tutorials for Keynote, Final Cut Pro, and Final Cut Express. Tutorials can be found at www. apple.com. Select support and then the program that you are using.

3

Conical

Stick Forts

Conical Stick Forts

Fort Focus: Some forts can get pretty pricey. Not this one! Conical stick forts were and can be made using just about any kind of sticks for the frame and any sort of brush or branches for the covering. These forts are fun to build, go up quickly and can lead to many imaginative hours of creative play.

Structure Story:

For most of human history, people made do with the natural building materials they could find. Rocks, branches, sticks, hides, large animal bones or whatever was around just might have become part of their homes! Can you imagine your house being made of stuff from around the neighborhood?

Not until modern transportation systems came about in the twentieth century were most people able to transport building materials over long distances. As most of us look at our homes today, we are probably looking at building supplies from other states, regions or even countries. Only recently have some people turned their attention back to local building materials due largely to the high cost of fuel associated with extracting and transporting raw and finished resources.

One interesting and almost universal building type, and one that lends itself to fort building, is the brush shelter or stick structure. These structures are known by many names. One name that is commonly used is wickiup. You can make these forts easily if you can gather just a few things!

Wickiups were temporary structures used mostly by hunter-gatherers who used available building materials and left the structure behind when they moved on to follow migrating prey or ripening plant foods. Some of these stick structures were conical in shape, using straight poles much like a tipi, but usually much smaller. Others were rounded using bent poles. Some of these rounded structures were actually inhabited for much longer periods of time. Some of the stick structures were built right into the side of a standing tree, taking advantage of its natural structural strength.

In Yellowstone National Park, historians have found stick structures still standing that were left behind by the Sheepeater band of the Shoshoni Indians of that region. Many a modern-day hunter has built a stick structure similar to a wickiup to aid them as they waited out a stormy night. One winter day not long ago, a group of young students in western Wyoming held class for more than two comfortable hours in a hastily built wickiup when they were caught in a snowstorm.

Stick structures are practical, fun to build and inexpensive to acquire. If they are damaged somehow, stick structures are easy to repair. Another nice thing about stick structures is that when you are finished with them, you can simply return the materials to the place where you found them.

A Story Activity: Think of the natural building materials available where you live. If you live in a city where those materials might not be available, find out what the land was like before the city was built. Design a structure in the space provided on the next page that uses some of those local materials. It doesn't have to be a stick structure; it just needs to be made of local stuff. Picture several wickiups together, and you have a village!

Activity Blueprint

Fort Journal: Keep a record of your fort building experiences on the Fort Journal pages at the end of this activity. On the journal pages, you can make notes, draw sketches, and attach photographs of your fort building experience.

A Model Idea: Build your model on a base of plywood or sheathing material. A large sheet will allow you to build a small village of structures if you choose to do so.

Conical Stick Structure: Wickiup

Materials
• Plywood or sheathing material 1/4" or thicker, 24" x 24" or larger.
• 5' jute twine
• An assortment of twenty or more short sticks about 8" long and the diameter of a pencil OR twenty 1/4" dowels cut to 8" lengths.
• One sheet of brown construction paper or small pieces of rawhide
• Tools: Scissors, low-temperature glue gun and glue sticks

Directions:

Step 1: Make the frame.

☑ Choose three of the straightest and strongest looking sticks. Measure each one, and make a mark 6 1/2" from the bottom.

☑ Lay the sticks side by side next to each other with the pencil marks lined up.

☑ Cut a 12" piece of string. Leaving the first two inches of string hanging free, weave the string over and around each of the three sticks at the pencil marks one time.   Stand the sticks up, and form a tripod shape. Continue to weave the string in a figure 8 over and around the sticks at the pencil marks.

When you have several inches of the string left, tie it in a tight knot together with the free-hanging end. You now have the basic wickiup frame.

Step 2: Attach the frame.

> Using the glue gun, glue each of the wickiup legs to the base. Draw a circle around the three tripod legs that are glued to the base.

Step 3: Build the structure.

> Place the remaining sticks so that the bottom of each stick is on the line and the top of the stick lies in the upper tripod crotch. Put one stick in each section, and continue to go around the frame adding one stick to each section until the crotches are full. Make sure to leave an opening on one side for the door.

> When the sticks are the way you want them, glue each stick to the base and at the top.

Step 4: Make the covering.

> Cut brown construction paper into 4" x 4" pieces. Crumple paper so that it looks like a worn animal hide, or select and cut rawhide pieces.

> Position the paper on the outer part of the structure, and attach it with glue to form a hide covering. Start laying paper or rawhide at the bottom and overlap on the sides and on top of one another. Do not cover the door opening.

Step 5: Complete the model.

> Make as many wickiups as you want in your village. Make pathways to the fort openings by lightly sketching path outlines with a pencil. Gently brush white glue inside the path outlines. Before the glue dries, sprinkle dry sand or dirt on it.

> Glue bushes, trees and other landscape details using materials like moss or small branches from your yard.

construction

A Child-Sized Fort

You are about to build one of the simplest and fun forts ever! Here is something to think about: this fort is made up of a series of triangular shapes. That is interesting because triangles are very strong. If you follow the instructions carefully, you will have a simple fort that will withstand many days of fun creative play.

In this fort, your imagination might take you to the steppes of Mongolia, the deserts of the American Southwest, the jungles of Africa, the rolling hills of Australia's Outback or the high country of the Rocky Mountains. As you use your imagination, this fort can transport you to different places and take you to different times!

Parent Tip: Help your child understand some basic construction tips for building this kind of structure:

- When carrying poles, be careful where the ends are pointing. You do not want to point them right into someone's eyes! Use teamwork, and have one buddy on each end to solve this problem.

- Make sure your rope is in good condition and that all knots are securely tightened.

Materials
• Twenty to thirty 1" – 2" diameter stick poles OR 2" x 2" boards from the lumberyard. (Not all of the poles need to be the same size. Your three tripod poles should be the largest diameter and the others can be much smaller. Decide how tall you want your structure to be at the high point on the inside. Add 2' to your pole lengths. If you want a fort that will be 6' tall in the center, make your poles 8' long.)
• Twenty feet of 3/16" or 1/4" nylon or manila rope
• Random branches or other brush with or without leaves
• Brown tarp for covering structure during the wet season
• Tools: Tape measure, scissors or knife for cutting rope

Directions:
Step 1: Select a fort location.

- Stick shelters work best on flat ground. Find a site that is relatively flat and at least 10' x 10' square.

- Clear debris, and make a space to the side for storing building materials.

Step 2: Gather materials.

❧ Get permission to gather fort materials. This was often the job of young people in cultures who used these structures.

Step 3: Assemble the tripod.

❧ Choose three of your strongest and straightest poles. Lay them side-by-side. Measure down 18" from the top and make a mark.

❧ Cut your twenty-foot length of rope in half.

❧ Fasten the tripod poles together with one 10' piece of rope at the places you marked on the poles. First, weave the rope between the first two poles and then weave the rope around the third pole. Cinch the rope tight.

❧ Go around the three poles two times and tighten as you go. Tie a simple knot here and leave the remaining rope loose.

Step 4: Stand the tripod upright.

❧ Get some help from a parent or another tall person for the next step. Stand the three tripod poles side-by-side with the tied end in the air. Position the three pole ends on the ground in the circumference of the fort. This will tighten the roped ends even more.

❧ Wrap the hanging rope end around the tripod tie rope, and tie another knot.

Step 5: Complete the frame.

❧ Look carefully at your tripod and see it as three distinct triangular sections. Choose one triangle to have the door opening. This will be triangle #1. Think of the others as triangle #2 and triangle #3.

❧ Create a circle on the ground around all three tripod pole ends. You could etch a circle in the soil using a stick or trickle sand or use chalk on a grassy area.

❧ Select another pole from your unused pole stack. In triangle #1 of the tripod, place one end of the pole on your circle line and nestle the other end in the crotch of the top of the tripod. Make sure it is secure. This will be one side of your door opening, so place it where you want that side of the door to be.

- Go to triangle #2, choose and place a pole as you did in triangle one.

- Go to triangle #3, and do the same.

- Go back to triangle #1 and place another pole. This will be the other side of the door opening, so make sure there is enough space between the two door poles to let you get in and out easily.Continue this process, going from triangle to triangle, until you have used all but six of your poles or the upper tripod crotches are full. Reminder: in triangle #1, do not cover the door opening with poles.

- Take the second 10' piece of rope and loop it around the tripod top encasing all of the poles. Cinch it tight and tie a knot when you have only a few feet left.

Step 6: Complete the walls.

- Place leafy branches or a brown tarp around the framework.

- Weave branches into others or tuck in the tarp.

- Lay the final six poles over the outer branches or tarp to help secure them.

- Your stick shelter fort is ready for play!

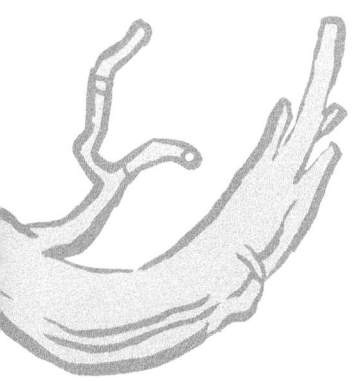

fortbuilder's journal

Stick Structure

Construction Dates:

My Plan: Make a building plan. Take photos of the site before you build, of gathering materials, of the people who will be helping and add them here.

Construction: Tell about what happened as you built. Did things go as planned? What was fun? What was hard? Add more photos and sketches. (You can use the space to the right as well.)

After Building: How have you used your new fort? What kinds of fun have you had? Write, draw, add photos and record the pleasures of having a fort!

Media Connection: Make a media journal to go along with your writing and sketches. Take photographs and create a photomontage or Keynote presentation. Record your fort building on video, and make a film of your experience using Final Cut Pro or Final Cut Express.

Post your media project on the Apple Student Gallery.

Review tutorials for Keynote, Final Cut Pro, and Final Cut Express. Tutorials can be found at www.apple.com. Select support and then the program that you are using.

4

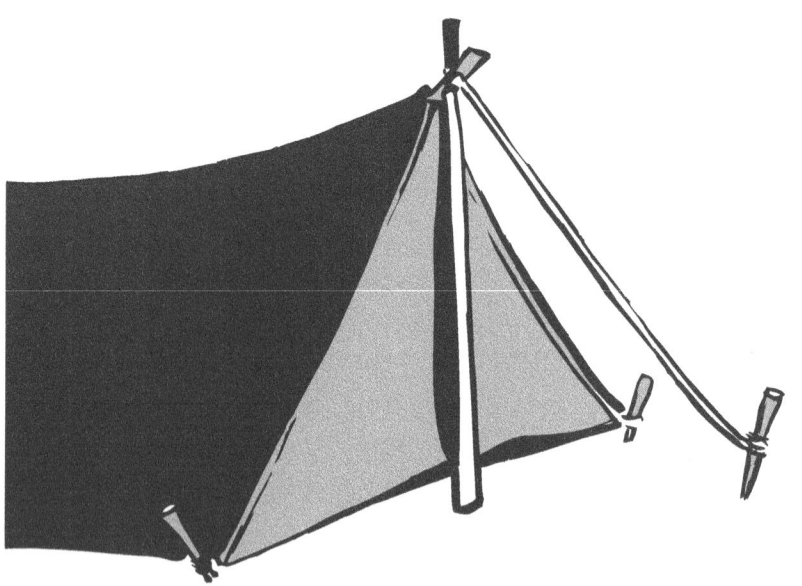

Tent Forts

Tent Forts

Fort Focus: Tent forts are some of the simplest and most fun forts to play with. This fort-building activity will help you learn how to construct several unique and portable forts in just a few minutes. Ready for tent-fort building? Read on!

Structure Story:

Many of us remember our first camping experience in a tent. We counted on those thin tent walls to protect us from the dark of night, the noises of the forest or the sounds of prowling animals! More than likely, those perceived dangers were nowhere nearby except in our tent-dweller imaginations.

Some of us remember tents built in the kitchen using chairs and blankets. Others remember turning their parents' work area using quilting frames, work benches, and gardening tables to make tent forts pretty quickly by simply covering the sides and crawling in.

Try this: Draw a picture of the first tent or tent fort you remember being in:

table structure is needed. Tent forts? You are about to make one!

A Story Activity: Tents come in many shapes, sizes and colors. Make a simple pop-up tent campground on the next two pages or on another sheet of paper. Here are the directions:

⌐ Cut out ten 3" x 3" pieces of blank white paper.

⌐ Use crayons or markers to decorate one side of each piece of paper in wild and creative ways. One might have blue and yellow polka dots; another might have pink and green stripes; and yet another might have star and moon shapes.

⌐ Now, fold the papers in half to create ten pup tents. The colored side should face up and out. Arrange the tents around the paper.

⌐ On each ten, fold a very small piece of one side of the paper so that you will have a small surface to glue the paper to the base. Use clear tape or a line from a glue stick to attach one of the two edges of each tent that touches the paper. Leave the other side loose so that the tents can fold flat when not in use. POP the tents back into position anytime you want your campground to reappear.

⌐ Draw roads, trails, rivers and lakes on the paper for your tent campground.

Background: Dictionaries define tents as portable shelters that are often made of canvas, nylon or plastic stretched over supporting poles or ropes and fastened to the ground.

Before moving on, get a world map or globe and find the Sahara Desert of North Africa. Imagine that you are a young nomadic child living in the Sahara Desert of North Africa 700–800 years ago. Your father may have been a trader who used camels— perhaps hundreds of them—to transport goods to trade with people who would use ocean-worthy ships to take his goods all over the known world. Your family, under your mother's guidance, would travel with the trade goods for months or years at a time. What did you live in? A tent! In fact, you always lived in a tent because, as no- mads, you were always on the move, and tent homes could be moved easily.

If you were going to live in a tent full time, what would you want it to be like? Draw a detailed picture of your dream tent above. Don't forget: tents are meant to be POR- TABLE shelters!

These days, tents are mostly used by campers and the military. They are also used for carnivals, circuses, and outdoor gatherings. You might find a tent anywhere a por-

Tent Forts

Activity Blueprint

Fort Journal: Keep a record of your fort building experiences on the Fort Journal pages at the end of this activity. On the journal pages, you can make notes, draw sketches, and attach photographs of your fort building experience.

Tent Fort Model Experiments

Materials
• Plywood or sheathing material 1/2" or thicker, 24" x 24" or larger
• A collection of pliable plastic sheets and paper that can be easily cut
• Short sticks and dowels with the diameter of a pencil or smaller
• White glue
• A roll of twine
• Tools: Scissors

Experiment with materials and create several unique tent models. Here are some ideas: pup tents, domed tents, pole tents, wall tents.

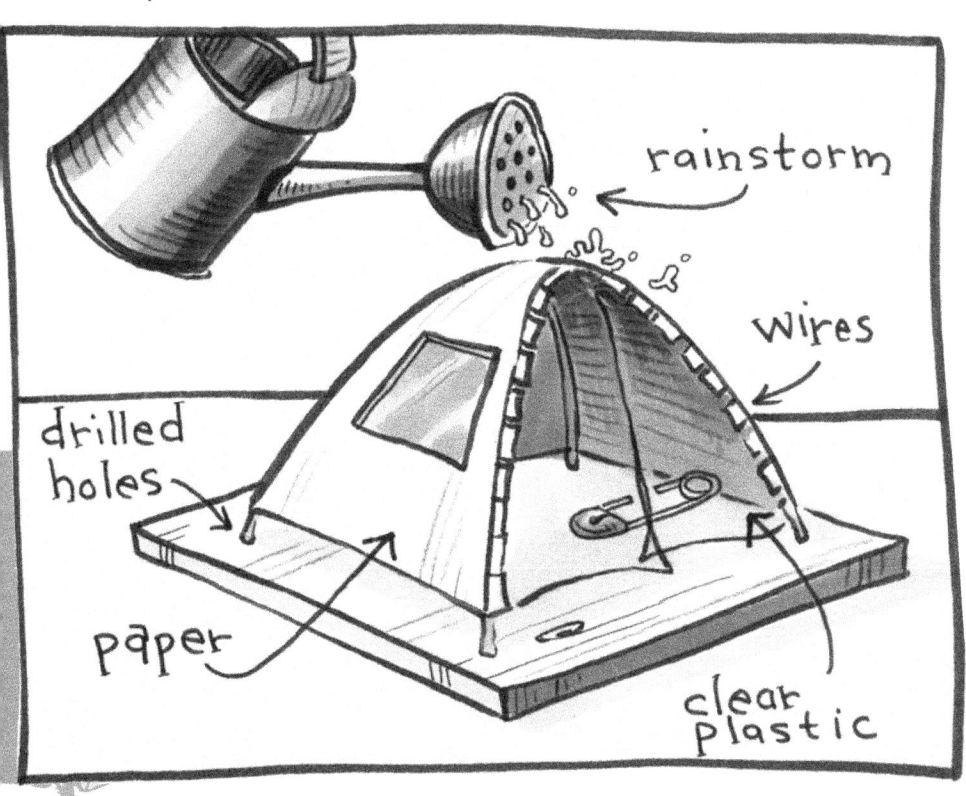

Do you need more ideas? Locate a camping supply catalog or find one on the Web, and see what they have to offer. Remember, tents are portable shelters that are often made of canvas, nylon or plastic stretched over supporting poles or ropes and fastened to the ground.

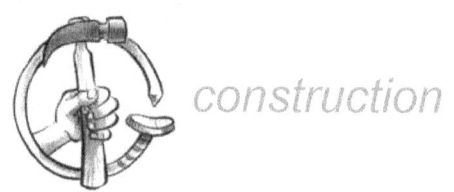 *construction*

Once you have created a tent that you like, attach it to your model base, and decorate the space around it in a way that fits its use.

A Child-Sized Fort

You will find ideas on how to construct several tent forts outlined here. Some are good for indoor forts, some for outdoors and others fit both locations.

Tent Fort #1: Chair Tent Fort

Materials
• A large blanket for the tent top
• Light blankets or sheets for the sides
• Clothespins
• 4 chairs

Directions:
Step 1: Place the chairs.

❧ Position the chairs so that the blanket or sheet stretches over all four chairs letting some of the blanket hang over the sides.

Step 2: Position the blankets.

❧ Secure the blanket corners together over the chair backs using clothespins. Gently place light blankets or sheets over the sides to form walls. Secure the sides with clothespins.

Step 3: Play in your chair tent fort.

❧ Bring in pillows, blankets, stuffed animals and friends, and pretend that you are camping. Chair tent forts are great places to read and look at books. Grab your iPod, lie back and enjoy some music. Use your chair tent fort as your base camp for climbing mountains and conquering unknown lands. Turn your chair tent fort into a sea-going ship headed for uncharted waters.

Tent Fort #2: Quick Tent Fort

Materials
• 20–50 feet of 3/16" – 1/4" rope
• Two 6'–8' tent poles
• 10' x 15' tarp or plastic
• Four–six large softball-sized rocks
• Ten clothes pins
• Tools: Measuring tape, black marker

Step 1: Locate a tent fort site.

❧ For this fort, you will need to be able to reach and attach your rope to two opposite points at a height of 5'–6'.

❧ Find a place that fits this description and is relatively flat. Option: Drive two 6'–8' poles into the ground at a distance of 20' from one another. Prepare the site by removing any obstacles.

Step 2: Set the support rope.

❧ Locate one point on the first pole that is 5'–6' from the ground, and mark that point.

🏹 Tie one end of your rope with a secure knot to the pole at the point you marked. Do the same on the opposite pole. Cinch the rope tight before securing the other end of the rope.

Step 3: Place the tent fort cover.

🏹 Measure the tarp or plastic along one edge of the 15-foot side, and place a mark at 7 1/2 feet. Measure the other 15-foot edge and place a mark at 7 1/2' feet. With a black marker, draw a line between the two 7 1/2 foot marks. This is the center line, or high point, of your tent roof.

🏹 Stretch the tarp or plastic over the rope, placing the center line directly on the rope. Secure the cover to the rope using ten clothespins spaced at even intervals along the rope.

Step 4: Secure the tent fort base.

🏹 Stretch one side of the tent to the ground making a triangular shape. Place half of your rocks on the edge of the cover to hold that edge down. Repeat the process with the other side.

Step 5: Use your quick tent fort.

🏹 These forts are great for imaginary play, camping trips and backyard sleepovers.

Imagine yourself as a North African nomad, a lost army sergeant living off the land or a traveling magician going from town-to-town in search of Merlin and King Arthur. Tired of this location? You can move and reset a quick tent fort in minutes now that you have experience!

Tent Fort #3: Pole Tent Fort

Materials
• Four 3-inch pieces of 1/8" rope
• One 2" x 2" x 8' pole that can be cut
• 20' x 20' tarp or plastic
• Four pre-made tent stakes or stakes made from wood scraps
• Tools: Tape measure, handsaw, hammer, shovel, black marker

Directions:
Step 1: Prepare your pole tent fort site.

☜ Locate a level site that measure at least 20' x 20' without obstructions. Locate the center of the site and dig a hole with a small diameter of at least 2" and about 1' deep.

Step 2: Place the center pole.

☜ Decide how tall you want your tent to be—up to a maximum height of 7 feet. Your pole should be 1 foot longer than the height of your tent. If you want a 6-foot high tent center, the pole should be 7 feet tall. Measure and cut the pole as needed.

☜ Place one end of the pole in the center hole that you dug. Replace the soil tamping it down firmly with your feet and hands. The pole should stand up by itself at this point but it is not truly secured yet.

Step 3: Position the tent cover.

☜ Find the exact middle of your tent cover. Lay the cover on the ground, and stretch it out completely. Use your tape measure or any other long, straight line and draw a line between opposite corners to mark the exact center of the cover as shown below.

☜ Using the same process, draw another line between the other two opposite corners. The center of the tent cover is where the two lines intersect. Make a large mark at that point.

☜ Have someone hold the center pole securely as you proceed. Place the cover

carefully over the pole with the center mark directly on top of the pole.

❧ Go to each corner, and grab a handful of tarp. Take one of your 3-foot pieces of rope, loop it around the gathered tarp and tie it tightly. Repeat the process with the other three corners.

❧ Drive a tent stake into the ground a short distance away from one tent corner. Tie the remaining rope to the stake. Repeat the process with the other corners while stretching the cover and securing to the stakes. Determine where your door opening should be, and make a 3-foot cut from the ground straight towards the center pole.

Step 4: Use your center pole tent fort.

❧ There is a lot you can do with this type of fort because of its size. Invite friends over to make up imaginary games and activities. Hold a sleepover inside your new fort.

Parent Tip: Rope is the perfect tool for children but they need to know basic rope safety rules such as never putting a rope around your neck, being careful with rope, and even some of those knots you learned back in your Girl or Boy Scout days.

Tent Fort

Construction Dates:

My Plan: Make a building plan. Take photos of the site before you build, of gathering materials, of the people who will be helping and add them here.

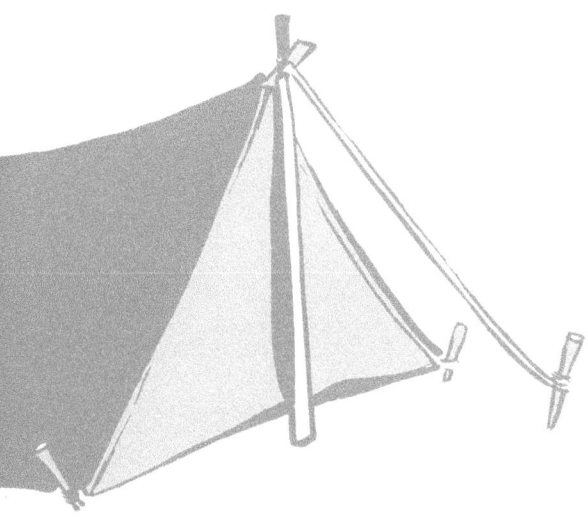

Construction: Tell about what happened as you built. Did things go as planned? What was fun? What was hard? Add more photos and sketches.

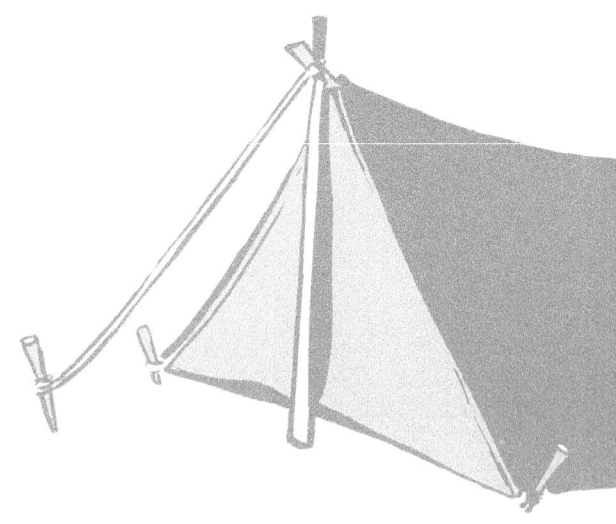

Tent Forts

After Building: How have you used your new fort? What kinds of fun have you had? Write, draw, add photos and record the pleasures of having a fort!

Media Connection: Make a media journal to go along with your writing and sketches. Take photographs and create a photomontage or Keynote presentation. Record your fort building on video, and make a film of your experience using Final Cut Pro or Final Cut Express.

Post your media project on the Apple Student Gallery.

Review tutorials for Keynote, Final Cut Pro, and Final Cut Express. Tutorials can be found at www. apple.com. Select support and then the program that you are using.

5

Lean-to Forts

Lean-to Forts

Fort Focus: A lean-to is a simple structure, easily made from common materials and fun to play in. Looking for a fort to play in today? This may be just the right choice!

Parent Tip: While the forts referred to in this activity are called lean-tos, they might more accurately, and more safely, be called lean-ons. Help your child find a safe location to lean support poles on rather than against.

Structure Story:

Imagine yourself as a wilderness traveler. Maybe you are in the bamboo forests of China, along a wooded riverbank in Argentina or roasting under the desert sun near an oasis in North Africa. The sun, wind or cold is starting to get to you after a long day, and your body is telling you to seek shelter. You look around you and into the distance, but there is no shelter to be found.

This is the situation many travelers have found themselves in for thousands of years of human history. Some travelers eventually located shelters. Others didn't and paid the price of exposure to the harsh elements. More than a few built a structure or fort that leaned against a low-hanging tree branch or rock face. Using any materials they could find, these travelers made lean-tos.

What's a lean-to? It's a shelter whose roof pitches in only one direction.

Draw a small picture of a lean-to in the space. below. It can be made of dried branches or conifer limbs that still have the needles attached. It could even be created from cactus branches! Be sure that the branches lean on something for support on the upper end, and that the other end rests on or near the ground.

When people have needed to put up a quick shelter, they searched for easily found building materials. Next, they looked for something to lean their shelter on. As you can see from the example above, lean-to frames create triangles, and triangles are known to be extra-strong when constructed properly. Properly built, a lean-to can stand a lot of wind or even snow.

The ground end of the lean-to can usually be counted on to give plenty of support. It is the upper end that must be considered. Actually, lean-tos often lean-on something for maximum support! Imagine resting the top of the lean-to sticks on a fence or a horizontal tree branch.

Once the lean-to fort is built, all kinds of exciting things can happen inside! As the rain pounds down, the sun roasts the outside world or the snow falls, people inside a lean-to might fix a meal, play a game or even travel in time to imaginary places to meet interesting people or creatures.

A Story Activity: In the space to the right, draw a map to an imaginary land that you decide to visit. Include details along the route. Show where dragons appear, enemy warriors approach, or a fairy princess lands on your shoulder. Use your imagination as you construct your map. Remember to show the location of the lean-to forts you build along the way!

Your Island Lean-to:

Map Name:

Activity Blueprint

Fort Journal: Keep a record of your fort building experiences on the Fort Journal pages at the end of this activity. On the journal pages, you can make notes, draw sketches, and attach photographs of your fort building experience.

A Model Idea: Build your models on a base of plywood or sheathing material.

A Lean-to Sampler

Materials
• Plywood or sheathing material 1/2" or thicker, 24"x 24" or larger
• An assortment of short sticks about the length and diameter of a pencil.
• Four 1/4" dowels cut to 8" lengths and three cut to 4 1/2" lengths.
• An assortment of small gravel-sized stones
• One rock about 4–5" high and 6–10" long and not too thick
• Tools: Low-temperature glue gun and glue sticks, drill and 1/4" drill bit, sand-paper

Directions:
Step 1: Make a structure to lean your models on.

How to build a simple post and pole fence model:

☇ Find the location for a 16" fence section on the model base. Drill three fence postholes 7 1/2 inches apart in a straight line. Do not drill all the way through the model base.

☇ Fit your four 1/2" dowels into the postholes. If they fit easily, then you are ready to move ahead. If they do not, lightly sand the end of the hole. Squirt a little glue from your glue gun into one hole and place a pole into it. Repeat with the other poles.

☇ Fasten two rows of horizontal poles to the fence posts as shown using glue to hold the poles in place:

How to make a model rock wall:

☇ Use your small gravel-sized stones. Glue a row of stones to the base in a 10 inch line.

Glue a second and third row of stones one on top of the other until your fence is about 4 inches high.

How to make a model stone cliff:

Place your rock on the base with the rock turned so that it gives you as much height and length as possible. Glue your rock in position.

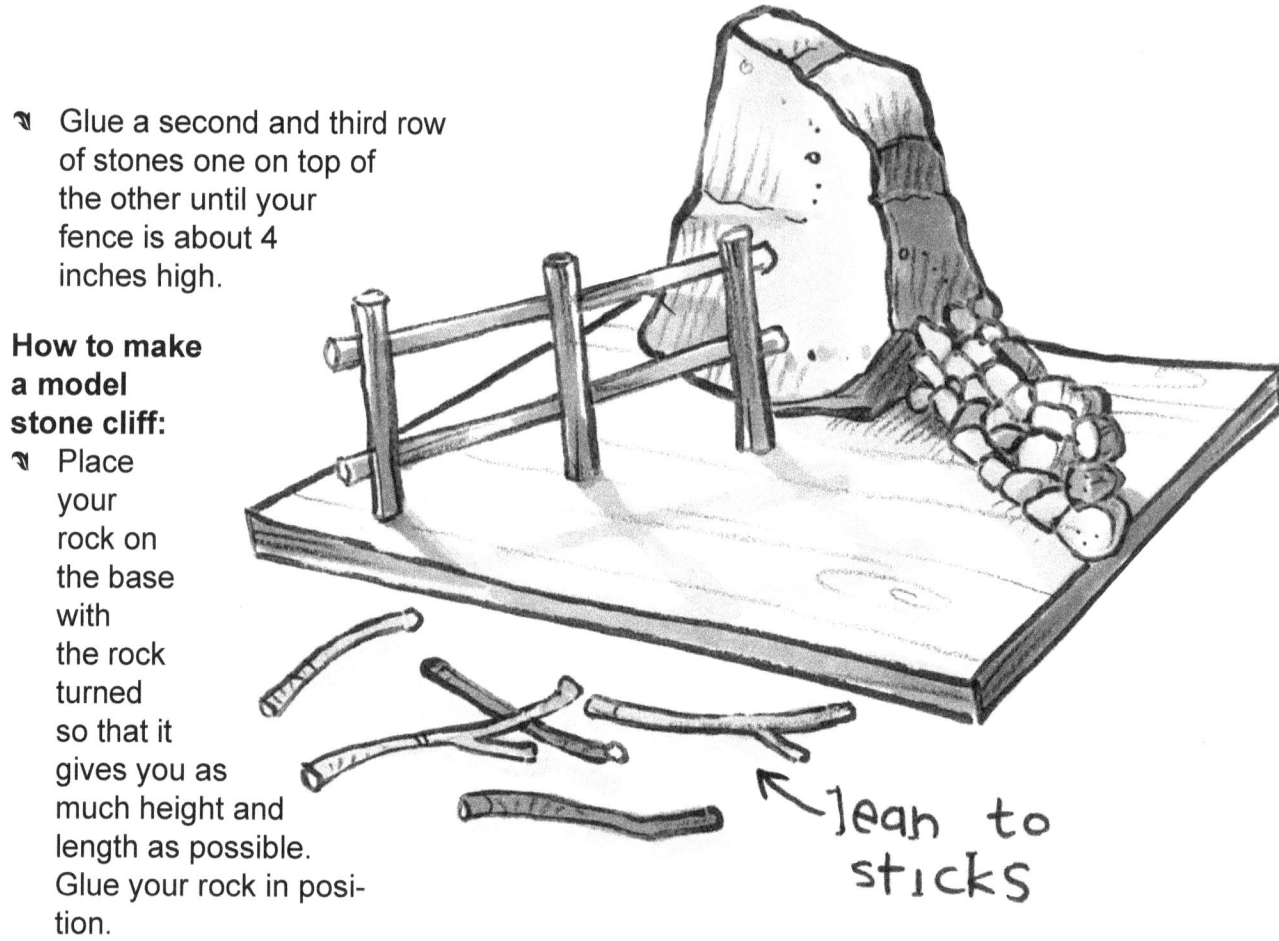

lean to sticks

Step 2: Build the lean-to structure.

Lay your sticks along a portion of the fence, rock wall or cliff with the tops of the sticks leaning on the structure and the bottoms on the base. The sticks should fit closely together.

When the sticks fit the way you want them, glue them in place. The structures should not cover the entire surface of your base. Place sticks horizontally on the lean-to poles from the ground to the top to create a more closed-in and protective roof.

Step 3: Complete the model.

Make pathways to the fort opening by lightly sketching path outlines with a pencil. Gently brush white glue within path outlines. Before the glue dries, sprinkle dry sand or dirt on glue.

Glue bushes, trees and other landscape details using materials like moss or small branches from around your yard. Add fire rings and other camp details.

construction

A Child-Sized Fort

The construction of this fort will go rapidly once you have gathered your materials and prepared your building site.

Materials
• An assortment of 8' sticks that are 1"–2" in diameter or 2" x 2" x 8' boards
• Note: The size of your lean-to will determine how many sticks you need.
• A tarp or branches with or without leaves or needles
• Twenty feet of 1/4" rope
• Tools: Shovel, tape measure

Directions:

Step 1: Identify and prepare the location.

◁ Have an adult help you find a suitable location for your fort. Look for a wall or other long surface that is tall enough to support your lean-to and sits on grass or dirt. Prepare the location by leveling the ground and removing obstacles.

◁ Starting at the wall or surface that you will use to lean your upper poles against, measure out 6 1/2 feet, and dig a 2" deep trench along a line that is parallel to the lean-to surface.

Step 2: Make your roof.

◁ Lay your support poles so that one end is in the 2" trench and the other is lying on the wall or support surface. As you put the poles in place, weave the rope under and over the middle point of the poles to tie the poles together.

◁ After all the support poles are in place, weave the rope back in the opposite direction. Wrap the rope on the opposite sides of the poles, as you weave so that each pole has rope wrapped on both sides. Tie off the rope at the end.

◁ Lay extra poles, branches, or the tarp over the support poles. These poles or branches should be in a horizontal position.

Step 3: Start playing.

◁ Make camp chairs, fire rings and other camp items to make your fort even more realistic.

Lean-to Forts

Construction Dates:

My Plan: Make a building plan. Take photos of the site before you build, of gathering materials, of the people who will be helping and add them here.

d

Construction: Tell about what happened as you built. Did things go as planned? What was fun? What was hard? Add more photos and sketches.

After Building: How have you used your new fort? What kinds of fun have you had? Write, draw, add photos and record the pleasures of having a fort!

Media Connection: Make a media journal to go along with your writing and sketches. Take photographs and create a photomontage or Keynote presentation. Record your fort building on video, and make a film of your experience using Final Cut Pro or Final Cut Express.

Post your media project on the Apple Student Gallery.

Review tutorials for Keynote, Final Cut Pro, and Final Cut Express. Tutorials can be found at www.apple.com. Select support and then the program that you are using.

Snow Forts

Snow Forts

Fort Focus: If you live in or visit a place where snow is found, then you just might want to build a snow fort. Snow forts are easy to build and require no special tools other than a shovel and warm clothes!

Structure Story:

For as long as humans and snow have been on earth together, there have probably been snow structures. The structures are used for emergency shelter, winter homes, camouflage and for fun.

Think of as many different snow structures you know of and draw simple sketches of them in the space to the left.

Igloos, or traditional snow shelters, built by Arctic-dwelling people for thousands of years are wellknown. Some Inuit people would build entire igloo villages. But igloos aren't the only snow structures.

Parent Tip: Snow forts should always be built and used under adult supervision. In the case of inexperienced snow forts builders, smaller is better!

Snow forts are primarily walls of snow built to protect oneself during a snowball fight. These forts are easy to make if snow conditions are right and, depending on the temperature, can last for a long time.

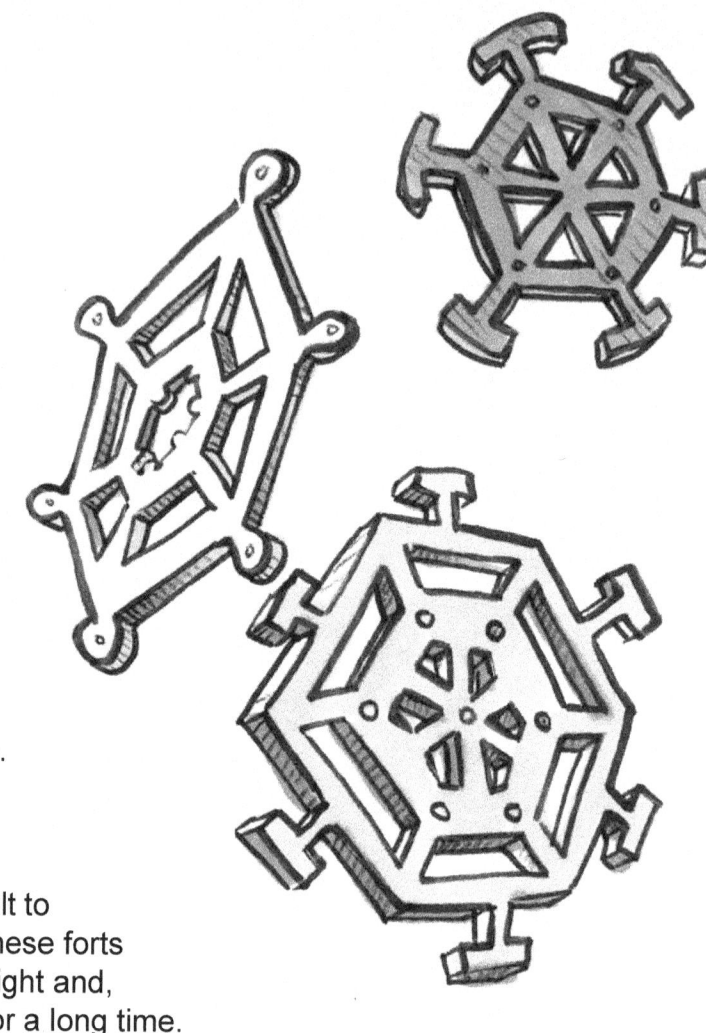

Ideal snow fort building conditions are when the outside temperature hovers somewhere near freezing. When it gets colder, the snow becomes granular and hard as the snowflakes lose their structure.

Even though snow forts can be easy to build, they require builders who have the proper winter gear and who know that they should never climb on or lean against a snow shelter because it is dangerous.

A Story Activity: Draw a map of a snow place where you spend time in the winter. It could be your backyard, a neighboring open space or a mountain area many miles away. Indicate places on your map where you would like to build a snow fort.

architect's model

Activity Blueprint

Fort Journal: Keep a record of your fort building experiences on the Fort Journal pages at the end of this activity. On the journal pages, you can make notes, draw sketches, and attach photographs of your fort building experience.

A Model Idea: Build your snow fort model on a base of plywood or sheathing material. Use this model to plan out the best places to put snow forts in your own neighborhood. You can do this on autumn days when you are looking at the sky and hoping that the real snow will start falling.

Snowball-Fight Forts

Materials
• Plywood or sheathing material 1/2" or thicker, 24" x 24" or larger
• White modeling clay
• Latex paints: white and earth-tones
• Tools: Low-temperature glue gun and glue sticks, paintbrush, small sponge or sponge brush

Directions:

Step 1: Prepare the model base.

↲ Paint a coat of white or earth-toned paint on the model surface.

↲ Use a small sponge to daub earth tones on first. After it dries, use the sponge to daub white paint if needed to give the surface a realistic look.

Step 2: Build the snowball fight model forts.

↲ Decide where you want to place two snowball-fight forts. Remember, at least two teams will have forts.

↲ Lightly draw the shape of your forts on the base. Each fort should be about as large as a small bowl.

❧ Make snowballs with clay about the size of a small piece of hard round bubble gum, and place them on the fort outline. Use a small amount of glue to attach each one to the base.

❧ Stack snowballs on top of one another until the fort is four or five snowballs high.

Step 3: Decorate the base, and have some fun.

❧ Add model details like trees, roads, people, houses, etc.

❧ There should be stacks of much smaller snowballs inside the fort ready for the snowball fight.

❧ Pretend that teams have really fun snowball fights!

A Child-Sized Fort

You can build real snow forts just like the models you built. You will need snow, of course, and time to build. Make sure you have proper outdoor clothing for extended outside work and play periods. Your snow conditions may dictate which style of fort you can build.

Parent Tip: Cotton clothing is never the best choice of material for prolonged outdoor time in winter. Hats that cover ears, warm and dry boots, good gloves or mittens and snow pants and jackets are a must. Dressing in layers of proper gear is often better than one thick layer that is either too hot or too cold.

Snowball-Fight Fort

Materials
• An ample supply of good "packing snow"
• Tools: Snow shovel

Directions:

Step 1: Choose and prepare the battlefield.

☃ Decide where you will locate your snowball-fight forts. Make sure trees, houses and other obstructions are not in the way.

☃ Use the heel of your boot or a stick to draw the outline of each fort in the snow.

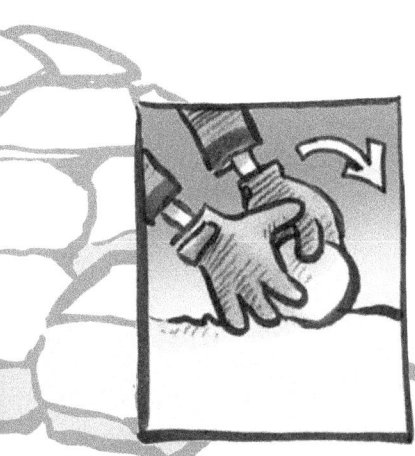  

Step 2: Build the forts.

❧ Make big, but manageable, snowballs by rolling smaller snowballs around to create the biggest snowball you can still move.

❧ Place these large snowballs around the base of the fort on the outlin you drew in the snow. Set the snowballs right next to each other and fill in gaps with snow. Leave an opening for the door if you are planning to have one.

❧ Make snowballs for the second row a little smaller than those on the first. Stack these snowballs much the same as the first row. Continue stacking rows of smaller snowballs until the walls are about four feet high.

Step 3: Using the snowball-fight fort.

❧ Caution: Do not lean, push, or stand on your snow fort walls.

❧ You may choose to just play inside the fort. There are all kinds of imaginative things you could do. If you decide to use yours for snowball fights, be sure to play fair, have fun and be smart!

❧ Throw snowballs, NOT ice balls. NEVER aim for the head area of your opponent. It's just for fun, so don't throw too hard. Stop when you are asked to do so. Establish rules that allow everyone to have fun in a safe way!

Snow Fort

Construction Dates:

My Plan: Make a building plan. Take photos of the site before you build, of gathering materials, of the people who will be helping and add them here.

Construction: Tell about what happened as you built. Did things go as planned? What was fun? What was hard? Add more photos and sketches.

After Building: How have you used your new fort? What kinds of fun have you had? Write, draw, add photos and record the pleasures of having a fort!

Media Connection: Make a media journal to go along with your writing and sketches. Take photographs and create a photomontage or Keynote presentation. Record your fort building on video, and make a film of your experience using Final Cut Pro or Final Cut Express.

Post your media project on the Apple Student Gallery.

Review tutorials for Keynote, Final Cut Pro, and Final Cut Express. Tutorials can be found at www. apple.com. Select support and then the program that you are using.

7

Wildlife-Viewing Forts

Wildlife Viewing Forts

Fort Focus: Everyone loves to observe wildlife. From backyard birds to frenzied squirrels to wandering deer, these and other animals have intrigued hunters and wildlife watchers for ages. The trick is how to hide our movements so as not to frighten animals away while at the same time not getting too close for the safety of animal or viewer.

The three wildlife viewing forts outlined in this activity range from simple to moderately difficult construction. All three can enhance your ability to watch and enjoy wildlife safely and conscientiously.

Parent Tip: Wildlife viewing is a fun and exciting learning experience. For some young people, it is their entryway into the world of collecting scientific field data. There are, however, safety issues to consider. Please talk to your child about the following: Avoid getting too close to wildlife. This can stress and frighten animals, which can make them unpredictable or defensive. Learn to watch an animal's behavior for clues that tell you to back off or stay away from them. Make observation periods brief. Never chase or handle wild animals no matter how cute or harmless they appear. Move quietly and slowly, and learn to communicate nonverbally with others.

Structure Story :

Somewhere along a rocky canyon ridge, a lone Nez Perce hunter sits silently behind a short wall of stone made by the ancestors for just this purpose. The young hunter knows that if he is patient and quiet, the elk that have come by this place as far back as memory recalls will come again. At his side, lying within easy reach, are his bow and arrows.

For two long days and nights he has waited. He knows that the rock wall hides his small movements from the ever-wary eyes and ears of his prey. That night, just hours before the elk return, the boy dreams of the ancestral hunters building the first stone wall, the one he sits next to now. In the dream, he realizes that their gift and the wall itself will help feed him and his family.

Imaginative Drawing: Draw a picture of the young hunter as he waits quietly behind his wall.

In another place, miles and ages away from the Nez Perce hunter, a young girl tries again and again to get close enough to her family's birdfeeder in order to really see

the details of her favorite bird's plumage. She creeps and moves along the ground looking more like an ancient hunter than a city birdwatcher. Once, when she got just close enough to notice the dark wing bands and buff-colored chest of her bird, she reached for her journal. The bird saw her movement and flew.

Dejected, the girl rose and walked to her house. As she wandered in to her bedroom, she almost tripped over the old refrigerator box her brother had been playing with. Frustrated with her brother, the birds and the box, she shoved the upright box against the window that overlooked the birdfeeder. Later, she noticed that every time she walked behind the big box, where the birds could not see her, they returned. And then an idea flew into her mind like autumn's migrating geese. She would turn the box into a bird blind—a bird viewing fort of sorts.

Her mom helped her place the box and cut some openings, and before an hour had *come and gone, our urban birdwatcher was exploring and recording her bird observations like never before.*

Imagine: What do you think her bird watching fort looked like sitting next to her bedroom window? Sketch a simple picture here:

What do you think she saw? In the binocular lenses below, draw two identical bird pictures. Use a field guide to help you with the details.

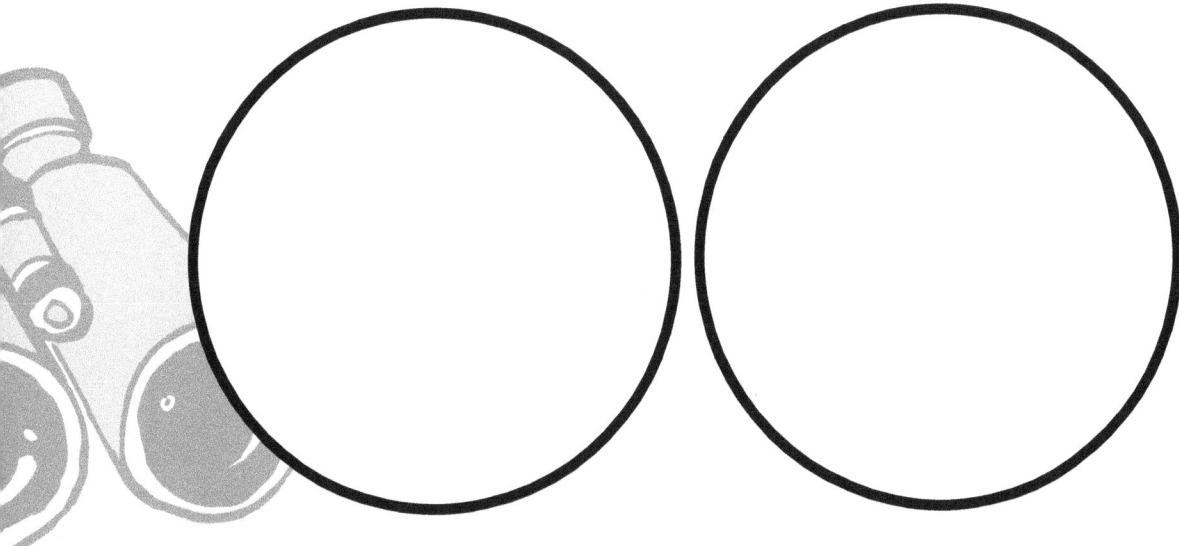

Getting close enough to view wildlife in a way that protects both the viewer and the viewed has been a human challenge for a long time. Blinds, a hiding place sometimes used by hunters or wildlife watchers, can and have been constructed out of a variety of materials. The one thing these blinds have in common is that they blend in with the surrounding area and provide a place where the viewers cannot be seen by wildlife. These blinds can be made into forts that work not only to enhance wildlife viewing but that can also be used for a variety of fun and playful activities.

A Story Activity: In the space below, draw a map or birds-eye-view of your yard, a local park where birds and squirrels hang out, or even a vacant lot nearby. After you place important details like buildings, trees, sidewalks and roads, indicate locations on the map where you have seen wildlife or think it might be found. Make a legend or key to help your map make sense.

architect's model

Activity Blueprint

Fort Journal: Keep a record of your fort building experiences on the Fort Journal pages at the end of this activity. On the journal pages, you can make notes, draw sketches, and attach photographs of your fort building experience.

A Model Idea: Build your models on a plywood or sheathing base.

Wildlife Viewing Fort Model #1: Stone Wall
Goal: To recreate the stone wall wildlife viewing fort of the Nez Perce Indian boy.

Materials
• Plywood or sheathing material 1/2" or thicker, 24" x 24" or larger.
• One cup of clean gravel stones for each wall
• Earth-toned latex paint and brushes
• Modeling clay or salt dough
• Optional: Small pre-made animal and human toy figures
• An assortment of small branches that look like leafless trees
• Tools: Low-temperature glue gun and glue sticks, drill and drill bit assortment

Directions:

Step 1: Identify wall locations.
- Look carefully at the model base, and decide if the model will include both the stone wall fort and the portable bird blind fort, or just the stone walls.

- Make light pencil marks on the base to indicate where the walls will be and where the other model will sit if it is going to share the same base. Each stone wall should be 4"–5" long.

Step 2: Build the stone walls.
- Decide which stones will be your base stones, and set them aside. Larger stones should form the base, and smaller stones should form the wall.

- Dribble a line of glue along one of your 4"–5" wall marks. Quickly set the rocks for the base of the wall side-by-side into the glue before the glue gets hard. Wait a minute for the glue to dry, and then begin setting the stones for the wall. Glue one wall stone at a time.

ᴪ You might want to leave small gaps between wall stones so that the viewer can see through the wall easily.

Step 3: Complete the model.

ᴪ Place and glue stones randomly around the model base to look like naturally scattered rocks. Use paint to create paths, trails, etc.

ᴪ Decide where trees will go. Place trees on the model by drilling a small hole the size of the trunk, inserting a small amount of glue and then the tree. Note: Do not drill all the way through the base.

ᴪ Add other details to make the landscape look realistic. Use clay or salt dough to create hills and mountains.

Step 4: Play with the model.

ᴪ Make animal and human figures with clay or use pre-made figures. Move figures around to act out different scenarios.

Wildlife Viewing Fort Model #2: Box Bird Blind

Goal: To make a model of a box turned into a bird blind for exciting backyard viewing.

Materials
Half-gallon milk carton, rectangular shape
Brown or tan construction paper: 1–2 sheets
Latex paint and brushes
Gravel and dry dirt
White glue
An assortment of small branches that look like leafless trees
Tools: Scissors, low-temperature glue gun and glue sticks, drill and drill bit assortment

Directions:

Step 1: Identify the location for the bird blind fort.

ᴪ Determine where you will place the bird blind fort on your model base, and put a light mark on the location.

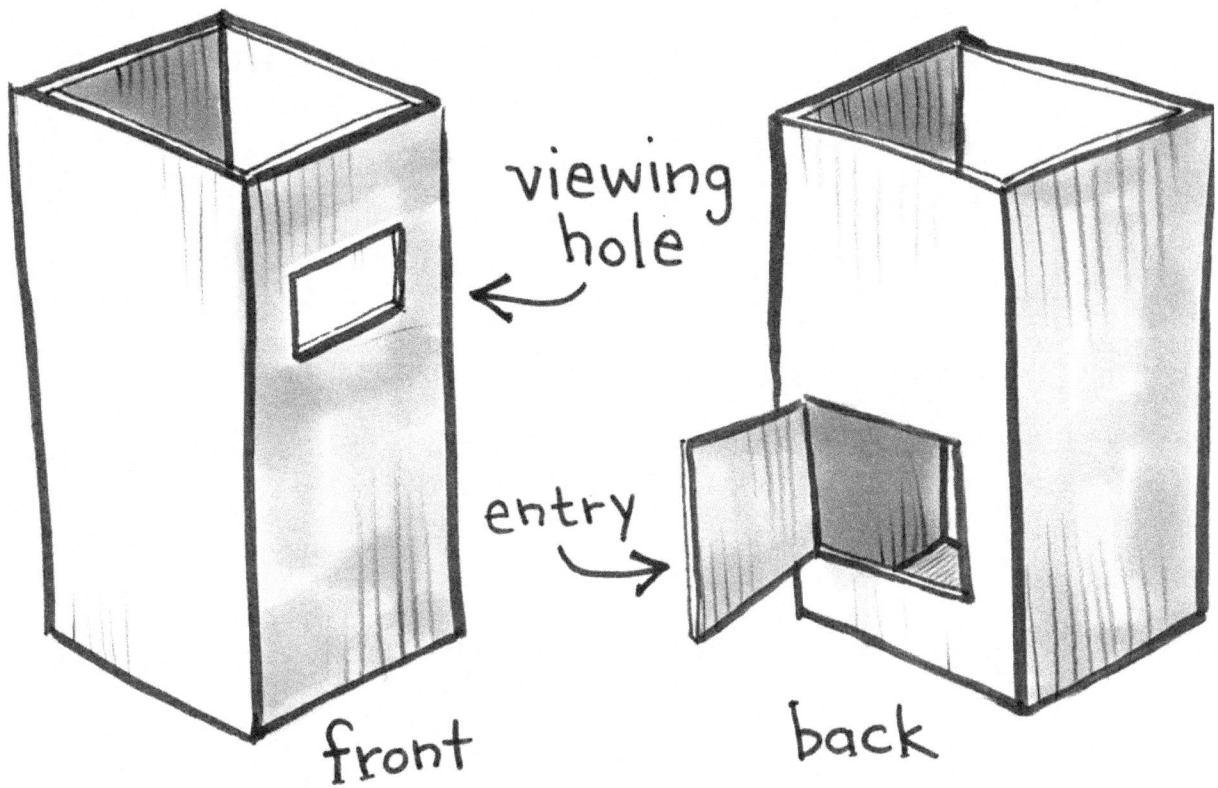

viewing hole

entry

front

back

Step 2: Prepare the blind.

❧ Wash and dry the carton inside and out.

❧ Cut off the top pouring-end of the carton, leaving four squared-off and even sides. Cut a viewing hole at eye-level on one side of the box as shown above. Cut an entry opening on the opposite side of the carton as shown above.

❧ Cover the outside of the blind with construction paper. Cut out viewing and entry holes and attach them to the carton with glue. Decorate the outside of the blind so that it is camouflaged to blend in with its surroundings.

Step 3: Complete the model.

❧ Glue soil on the model base to look like a backyard. Use paint to create sidewalks, driveways, lawns, etc.

❧ Decide where trees will go. Most of your model trees should be taller than your bird blind box. To place trees on the model, drill a small hole the size of the trunk, insert a small amount of glue in the hole, then insert the tree. Do not drill all the way through the base. Add other details to make the yard look realistic, such as fences, swing-sets, and other elements.

Step 4: Play with the model.

❧ Make animal and human figures with clay or use pre-made figures. Move figures around to act out different scenarios. Add toy cars and trucks to the scene.

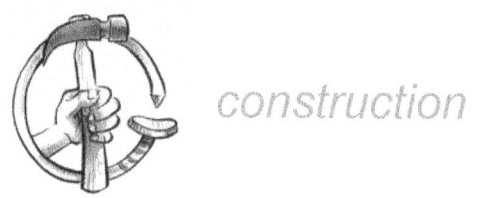

construction

A Child-Sized Fort

Wildlife Viewing Fort #1: Portable Bird Blind

Parent Tip: Be ready to help your child cut heavy cardboard with a heavy-duty utility knife. This should be done by you or under your supervision.

Materials
• Large heavy cardboard refrigerator box
• Exterior latex paint: neutral color for overall box and camouflage colors
• Clear plastic sheet that is 4 mil or thicker for the roof
• Tools: Utility knife, paintbrushes

Directions:

Step 1: Prepare the box.
- Remove the top of the box, leaving four evenly squared-off walls OR cut an opening in the top to create a skylight. Leave the bottom intact to provide support for your fort's shape.

- Cut a viewing hole at eye-level on one side of the box as shown to the right. Cut an entry opening on the opposite side of the box as shown to the right. *Tip: If you want to have an actual door, do not cut one of the sides. Hinge your door along that side by bending the cardboard back and forth.*

- Paint the outside of the blind with a neutral base paint using exterior latex paint. Allow the paint to dry before proceeding.

- Decorate the outside of the blind so that it looks camouflaged to blend in with its surroundings. Paint leaves or camouflage patterns on the base-coat of paint. Attach clear plastic to the top of the box to prevent rain or snow from getting inside.

Parent Tip: Help your child identify suitable and acceptable portable wildlife viewing fort locations.

Step 2: Use your portable bird blind fort.
- Decide if you will place the fort outdoors or next to an indoor window that has a good view of a birdfeeder.

- Stabilize the fort. If you are using your fort outdoors, drive tent stakes through the floor of the box and into the soil. Tacks or masking tape can be used to attach the blind to an indoor window frame.

- Supply the fort. A sitting stool, bird field guide, observation journal and binoculars can add a great deal to this fort.

Step 3: Spend time and be patient.
- It may take birds a while to get used to their new neighbor. Take a book along, and just enjoy some quiet time while you wait.

Wildlife Viewing Fort #2: Temporary Wall Fort

Parent Tip: Help students stack their blocks so that safety and structural integrity issues can be discussed.

Materials
• Seventeen 6" x 8" x 16" cinderblocks (full blocks)
• Four 6" x 8" x 8" cinderblocks (half blocks)
• One 1" x 6" x 8' board
• Tools: Handsaw, tape measure

Directions:
Step 1: Prepare the location.
- You will need a level space where you can build a 6 1/2 foot wall. Choose a location that looks over an area where wildlife can be found, such as a field, a vacant lot, or an area with trees. Level the area as needed.

Step 2: Build the wall fort.
- Place five 6" x 8" x 16" cinderblocks side-by-side.

- Place a half block on one end of the second row. Next, place four full blocks side by side. Complete the row by adding one more half block to the end.

- Begin the third row with a full block, and then a half block from one end. Working from the other end, place two full blocks and then a half block.

- This should leave a viewing space as pictured on the next page.

- Measure the wall, and cut the eight-foot board to that length. Lay the board on top of the third row.

🗸 Finally, lay five full blocks side-by-side on top of the board to complete the wall.

Step 3: Use the temporary wall fort.

Parent Tip: These temporary wall forts should not be played on. Review safety rules for the fort with your child.

🗸 Get behind the wall and use the viewing hole for watching wildlife. Peek around the top and edges for views as well.

🗸 Lay a blanket or pad on the ground for comfort as you lie and kneel in your fort.

🗸 Bring field guides, observation journals, binoculars and other tools to help with your viewing experience.

🗸 Rebuild the wall in another location to watch different wildlife.

Wildlife Viewing Fort

Construction Dates:

My Plan: Make a building plan. Take photos of the site before you build, of gathering materials, of the people who will be helping and add them here.

Construction: Tell about what happened as you built. Did things go as planned? What was fun? What was hard? Add more photos and sketches.

After Building: How have you used your new fort? What kinds of fun have you had? Write, draw, add photos and record the pleasures of having a fort!

Media Connection: Make a media journal to go along with your writing and sketches. Take photographs and create a photomontage or Keynote presentation. Record your fort building on video, and make a film of your experience using Final Cut Pro or Final Cut Express.

Post your media project on the Apple Student Gallery.

Review tutorials for Keynote, Final Cut Pro, and Final Cut Express. Tutorials can be found at www. apple.com. Select support and then the program that you are using.

8

Garden Forts

Garden Fort

Fort Focus: Gardening is a passion for many adults. Some children get to spend time in the garden, too, but some find the garden uninteresting or off-limits. Here is a fort idea that combines the love of fort building with gardening in a pleasing and ever-changing way!

Parent Tip: Garden forts will place your child in proximity with bees and other insects. Be prepared for any allergies that might occur from working in the garden.

Structure Story :

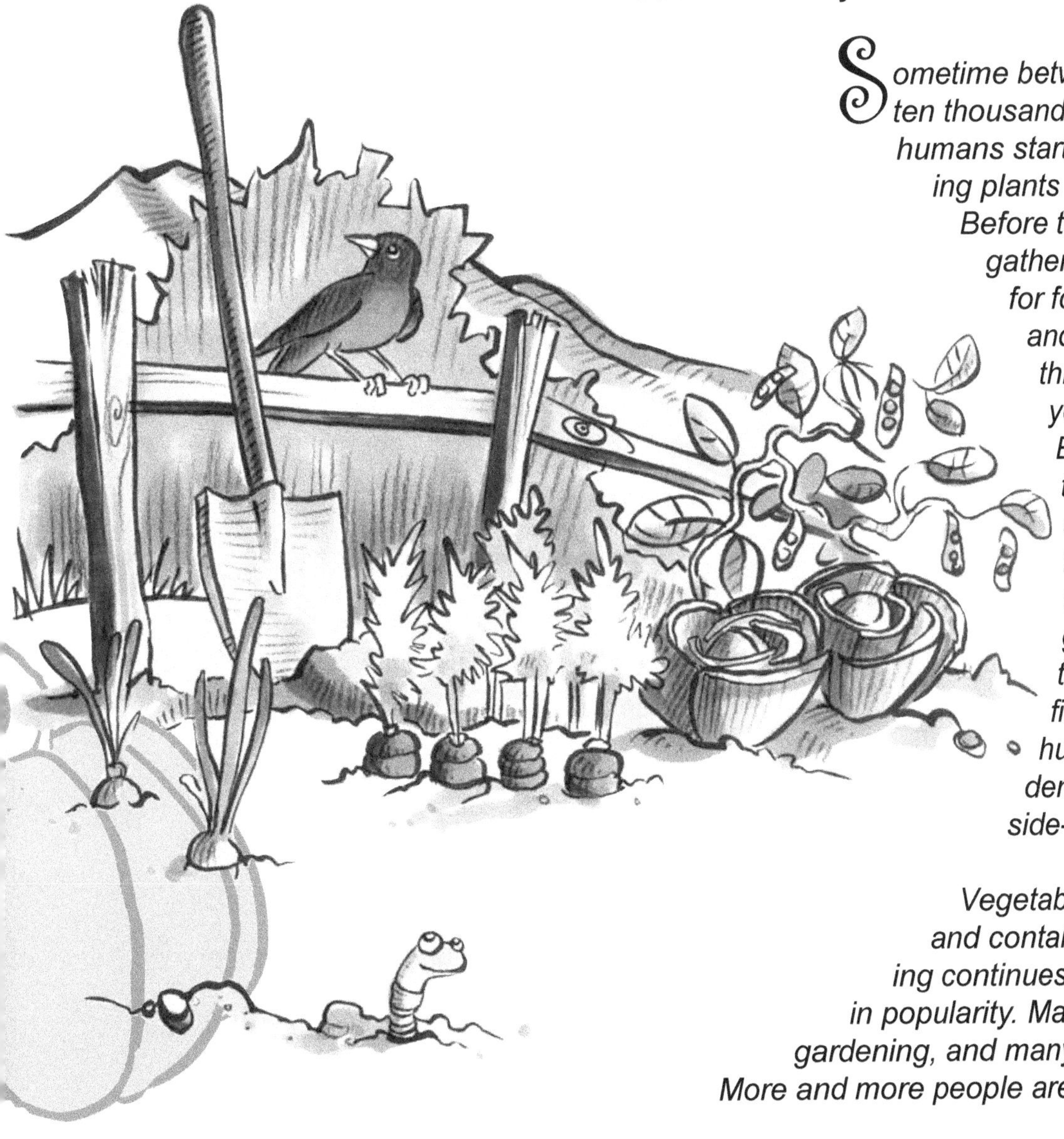

Sometime between five and ten thousand years ago, humans started cultivating plants for their use. Before that, they gathered wild crops for food, clothing and shelter. About three thousand years ago in Egypt, it seems that ponds and fruit trees began to show up in walled gardens. From the time of the first garden, humans and gardens have grown side-by-side.

Vegetable, ornamental and container gardening continues to increase in popularity. Many adults love gardening, and many kids do, too! More and more people are starting to *play in and around their gardens. Gardens are not just a fenced-off part of the yard or property anymore. For many families, they are an important part of the landscape.*

Why do kids love gardens? Maybe it's because there is dirt, growing things, water and sometimes food. That's a pretty good combination. Besides, if you are going to be a gardener, you just have to get dirty!

What do gardens and forts have to do with one another? If you like them both, here is a chance to combine your interests. Just think: if your family garden included a fort, it would provide a place to grow food and flowers and an exciting place to play and learn.

A Story Activity: Where do you live? Maybe you live in the desert, a subtropical landscape, in the mountains, along the ocean or in a heavily wooded area. Draw a picture that shows a typical garden in your area. If you don't have a garden, go for a walk, find one and sketch it here. Do you have a favorite garden plant? Sketch it, too!

architect's model

Activity Blueprint

Fort Journal: Keep a record of your fort building experiences on the Fort Journal pages at the end of this activity. On the journal pages, you can make notes, draw sketches, and attach photographs of your fort building experience.

A Model Idea: Build your models on a plywood or sheathing material base.

Garden Fort Model

Materials
• Plywood or sheathing material 1/2" or thicker and 24" x 24" or larger
• Pencil
• Colored paper
• One sheet of 4" x 4" cardboard, heavy cardstock or poster board
• Markers
• White glue
• Earth-toned latex paint
• One cup of dry soil

Directions:

Step 1: Create your garden.

❧ Paint a coat of light or earth-toned paint on the base for your model. When the paint has dried, lightly sketch a design including all the features including various garden beds, paths, birdbaths, and benches.

❧ Use earth-toned paint or real dirt for your garden beds and dirt paths. Brush a coat of glue on the base where you want soil to stick, and sprinkle dry soil on the glue. Remove excess soil by blowing lightly on it after the glue has set.

❧ To represent the plants, use one or more of the following techniques: Paint different colors representing different types of plants in the garden beds. Cut out plant shapes from colored paper and glue them to the base. Collect dried plant material from your yard and glue them to the base.

❧ For other garden details, make or find items that are the right size for your model.

Draw outlines of benches, birdbaths, and other items. Cut out magazine photos, and glue the photos on the base.

Step 2: Experiment with the fort location.

- Use the 4" x 4" piece of cardboard to represent your proposed garden fort. Move the piece from place to place on your model to see how it fits, what needs to be changed, and how it will enhance the garden.

Step 3: Share your fort idea.

- Propose two or more locations for your garden fort to your parents. Use the garden model as a visual aid.

Step 4: Place your fort on the model base.

- After you and your parents decide on a garden fort location, make a 4" x 4" replica of your fort, and attach it to your model base.

A Child-Sized Fort

Depending on where you live, a garden fort can be used year-round. If you live in a place where the gardening season is spring through fall, you can use your garden fort easily during those months. *(See a finished version of the fort on the following page.)*

Materials
• Lumber: four 2" x 2" x 4'; four 2" x 2" x 5'; four 2" x 2" x 6'
• 16–18 gauge galvanized lumber connectors
• One pound of 1 1/2" flathead grabber screws
• Seventeen feet of 48" garden fencing
• One-half pound of fence staples
• Twenty 1" x 2" x 6' boards: optional
• Climbing plants
• Tools: Phillip's screwdriver, wire cutters, hammer, garden tools

Directions:

Step 1: Prepare the location.

⚐ Your garden fort will be 4' high and measure 5' x 6' at the base, so prepare a location that has plenty of room for your fort and for your garden beds.

Step 2: Build the frame.

⚐ Use galvanized lumber connectors to fasten the lumber together to create a frame that is 4' tall x 5' wide x 6' long

⚐ Place the fort frame in position in the garden.

Step 3: Place wire covering on the sides of the fort.

⚐ Decide which end will be the fort entry. Cover the other three sides of the fort with garden wire and fasten it with fence staples.

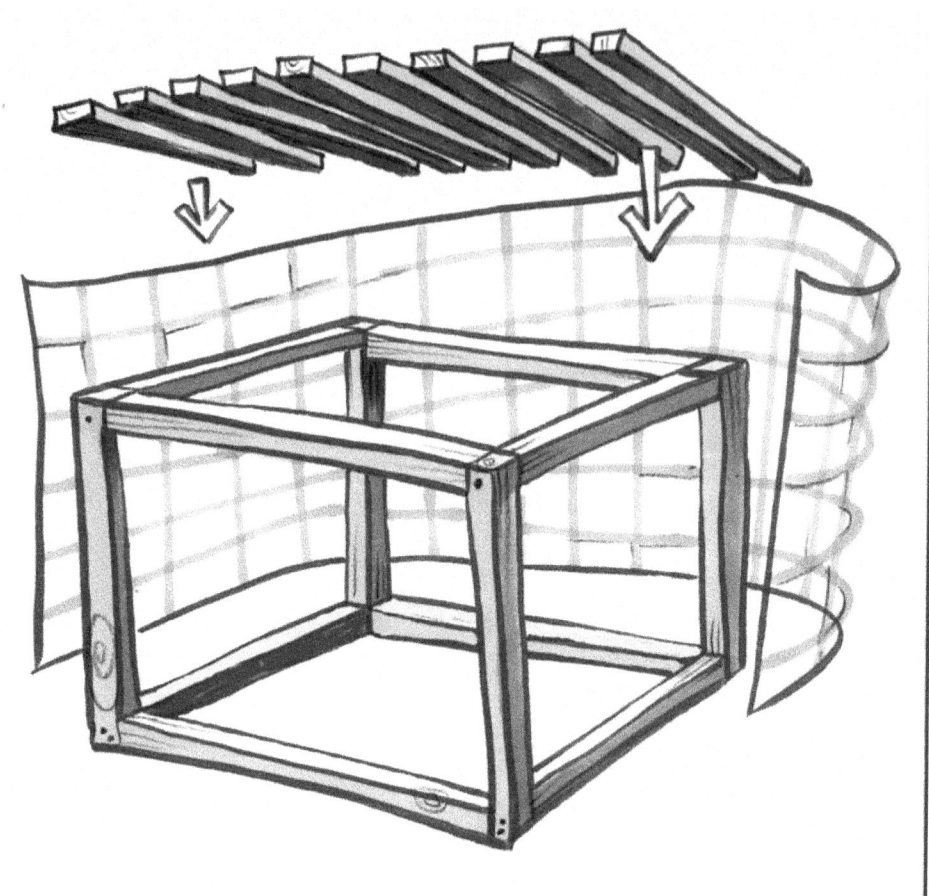

Step 4: Add a roof to your fort. (Optional)

❧ Place 1" x 2" x 6' boards on the roof so that six inches hang over each side.

❧ Leave a 2 1/2" – 3" space between boards.

❧ Fasten to the top with one 1 1/2" screw in each end to top rail.

Step 5: Plant climbing plants next to your fort.

❧ Prepare garden areas on three sides of the fort for planting.

❧ Purchase climbing plants or seeds for climbing plants and plant them according to instructions. Some climbing varieties are chocolate vine, morning glory, climbing hydrangea, clematis, trumpet vine, blac-eyed Susan vine and canary creeper. Check with your local nursery for advice on what plants grow best in your area.

Step 6: Use your fort.

❧ Decorate the inside of the fort, build pathways to it and enjoy your garden privacy.

❧ In the fall when plants are finished, cut corn stalks and lay them against the outside wall of your fort to give some autumn privacy.

⌐ Place a tarp over the top when autumn rains begin. Be sure to remove it when snow season arrives.

Parent Tip: By inviting your child into the garden you may be inviting gardening into their lives for many years to come.

Garden Fort

Construction Dates:

My Plan: Make a building plan. Take photos of the site before you build, of gathering materials, of the people who will be helping and add them here.

Construction: Tell about what happened as you built. Did things go as planned? What was fun? What was hard? Add more photos and sketches.

After Building: How have you used your new fort? What kinds of fun have you had? Write, draw, add photos and record the pleasures of having a fort!

Media Connection: Make a media journal to go along with your writing and sketches. Take photographs and create a photomontage or Keynote presentation. Record your fort building on video, and make a film of your experience using Final Cut Pro or Final Cut Express.

Post your media project on the Apple Student Gallery.

Review tutorials for Keynote, Final Cut Pro, and Final Cut Express. Tutorials can be found at www. apple.com. Select support and then the program that you are using.

9

Fairy Forts

Fairy Forts

Fort Focus: Fairies are very popular today as they have been for thousands of years. Children, little people themselves, are especially drawn to fairies. Learn to build several fairy fort models and one structure large enough for the child-sized fairy of today to play in and enjoy for a long, long time!

Structure Story :

Dictionaries tell us that fairies are imaginary beings that look like tiny humans and who are mischievous, clever and have magical powers. There are many stories, some very old, that feature fairies.

What do you think fairies look like? Draw one in the space to the right:

In Ireland, Scotland and Wales, stories of magical little people have been associated with power, danger and magic. However, stories of magical little people are not just a European concept. People from all over the world tell stories of others who live side-by-side with humans and who seem to have something special about them.

Do you have any books about fairies? List them here. Go to your local library or bookseller to see if they have any books that feature fairies. Write the titles here, and mark one that you would like to read.

_____

_____

_____

_____

Different people see fairy forts in different ways. No matter what form the historic structure takes, it may be seen as somewhat magical and, if it is not off-limits, it is not to be altered. Fairy forts can be found throughout the British Isles. Sometimes they are made of large stones that create a sort of cave-like opening. Sometimes they are mounds of earth that appear to have been burrowed into and the area looks somewhat like a prairie dog town. Some are circular spaces largely covered with dirt that hide ruins of ancient Celtic houses protected by the magic of Druids. One kind of fairy fort is the area found between a circle of trees growing closely together.

Are fairies real, and do fairy forts really exist? That's up to you to decide, but if you have an imagination and like the idea of playing host to fairies or to imagine that you are one of the magical little people yourself, building a fairy fort or fairy fort model could be lots of fun!

A Story Activity: In the space on the next page, draw a picture of one or more of the styles of fairy forts mentioned in the story: large stones that create a sort of cave-like opening; mounds of earth that appear to have been burrowed into; circular spaces largely covered with dirt that hide ruins of ancient Celtic houses; and circles of trees growing closely together.

Fortbuilders

architect's model

Activity Blueprints

Fort Journal: Keep a record of your fort building experiences on the Fort Journal pages at the end of this activity. On the journal pages, you can make notes, draw sketches, and attach photographs of your fort building experience.

Parent Tip: Some or all phases of the model building outlined below may require your supervision.

Fairy Fort #1: Stone Dolman

Materials

- Plywood or sheathing material 1/2" or thicker, 24" x 24" or larger piece for base
- Earth-tone latex paint for base
- Low-temperature glue gun and glue sticks
- White glue
- Foam paintbrush
- Assortment of small rocks with a surface area of 2" x 2" to 6" x 6" and a thickness up to 1"
- Small gravel-sized stones, dry dirt or sand and other natural materials for base

Directions:

Step 1: Prepare the base.
- Paint the base with an earth-tone latex paint, and let it dry.

Step 2: Build the fort.
- Decide which rocks will become the support rocks for the cave. You will need two or three. Arrange them on the base, and make sure that you have a roof rock that will span the space between support rocks. If not, get a larger roof rock or move your support rocks closer together.

- Make a mark where each support rock goes. With your glue gun, place an appropriately sized glob of glue on the base, and set your first support rock in the glue before it dries. Repeat the process with each support rock.

- Place another glob of glue on the top of each support rock to attach the roof rock. Quickly position the roof rock in the glue before it hardens.

Step 3: Complete the model.
- Make pathways to the fort opening(s) by lightly sketching path outlines with a pencil. Gently brush white glue within path outlines. Sprinkle dry sand or dirt on the glue before it dries.

- Glue bushes, trees and other landscape details using materials such as moss or small branches from around your yard.

Fairy Fort #2: Earth Mound

Materials
• Plywood or sheathing material 1/2" or thicker, 24" x 24" or larger piece for base
• Earth-tone latex paint for base
• Low-temperature glue gun and glue sticks
• White glue
• Foam paintbrush
• Modeling clay
• Dry dirt
• Small gravel-sized stones, dry dirt or sand and other natural materials for base

Directions:

Step 1: Prepare the base.
- Paint the base with an earth-tone latex paint, and let it dry.

Idea: Design a soda straw hinge for the door that pivots on a wire embedded in the clay.

Step 2: Build the fort.

ᐅ Create the earth mound from modeling clay. Make an entry opening on one side of the mound. Make a smaller escape opening on the other side of the mound.

ᐅ When the clay is dry, decide where to place the fort on the base. Trace lightly around the clay with a pencil.

ᐅ With the glue gun, place globs of glue within the traced area. Place the clay mound on the glue before it dries.

ᐅ Brush white glue on the outside surface of the clay. Sprinkle dry dirt on the glue before it dries.

Step 3: Complete the model.

ᐅ Make pathways to the fort opening(s) by lightly sketching the path outlines with a pencil. Gently brush white glue within path outlines.

ᐅ Sprinkle dry sand or dirt on the glue before it dries.

ᐅ Glue bushes, trees and other landscape details using materials such as moss or small branches from around your yard.

Fairy Fort #3: Celtic Ruins

Materials
• Plywood or sheathing material 1/2" or thicker, 24" x 24" or larger piece for base
• Earth-tone latex paint for base
• Low-temperature glue gun and glue sticks
• White glue
• Foam paintbrush
• Modeling clay
• Dry dirt
• Small gravel-sized stones, dry dirt or sand and other natural materials for base

Directions:

Step 1: Prepare the base.

❧ Paint the base with earth-tone latex paint, and let it dry.

Step 2: Build the fort.

❧ Decide where you want to place your fort on the base. Draw a light pencil line creating a rectangle about 10" x 16". This is the outline of your Celtic ruin. To create the foundation for your ruin, use your glue gun to glue small stones on the lines that you drew.

❧ Each stone should touch the stone next to it. This creates the foundation of your ruin. Glue a second tier of stones randomly around on top of the foundation.

❧ Shape modeling clay into an earth mound that is the right size to fit in the center of the ruin. Make an entry opening on one side.

❧ Make a smaller escape opening on the other side of the mound. When the clay is dry, place it in the center of the ruin.

❧ Trace lightly around the clay with a pencil. Use the glue gun to place globs of glue inside the traced area. Before the glue hardens, place the clay mound on the glue globs.

❧ Brush white glue on the outside surface of the clay; over the base within the ruin; over the rocks; and slightly outside of the ruin. Before the glue dries, sprinkle dry dirt on the glue.

Step 3: Complete the model.

❧ Make pathways to the fort openings by lightly sketching path outlines with a pencil. Gently brush white glue within path outlines. Before the glue dries, sprinkle dry sand or dirt on glue.

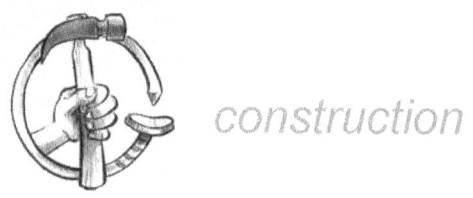

construction

A Child-Sized Fort

This really fun fort is meant to be played in, NOT played on! Let the real fairies cavort on top, and you can have the inside for yourself. Also, keep the door opening open at all times. When the exterior is completed, decorate the inside with anything that makes the space seem magical.

Parent Tip: This fort-building project requires the use of tools that require adult supervision.

Materials

- 1/2" or thicker sheet of exterior plywood or sheathing material
- Two pieces 3' x 5'
- Two pieces 3' x 3'
- 5/8" or thicker 4' x 6' sheet of exterior plywood or sheathing material
- Four 2" x 2" x 3' boards
- 1 1/2" flathead wood screws
- Exterior paint or wood preservative
- One pint exterior gray paint
- Black large-tip permanent marker
- Dirt
- White glue
- Tools: Handsaw, jigsaw, Phillip's screwdriver, shovel, wheelbarrow, foam brush

Directions:

Step 1: Find a location for your fort.

❧ Locate a flat area at least 6' x 6', and level the space as needed.

Step 2: Build the interior walls.

❧ Use the jigsaw to cut a half-round door in one of the 3' x 3' panels.

❧ Place a 2" x 2" x 3' board along each three-foot side of a 3' x 5' panel.

❧ Use four to six 1 1/2" screws to attach the board to the panel edge. Screw from the

plywood side into the panel and then into the 2"x 2". Repeat with the other 3' x 5' panel.

❧ Stand each 3' x 5' panel parallel to one another and 3' apart. You will need help holding these in place.

❧ Use four to six 1 1/2" screws to attach the solid 3' x 3' panel to the 2" x 2" board on the 3'x'5' panel. Repeat with the 3' x 3' panel with the door opening.

❧ Paint the surfaces with exterior paint or wood preservative.

Step 3: Build the roof.

❧ Take the 4' x 6' sheet, and draw a line around its perimeter creating an uneven edge that gives the appearance of a large stone.

❧ Make sure to keep the inside of the lined surface larger than 3 1/2' x 4 1/2'.

❧ Cut along the line with the jigsaw.

❧ Paint the upper surface with gray exterior paint. When the paint is dry, use the permanent marker to create light lines that look like cracks or uneven surfaces in the stone slab.

Step 4: Place the fort in its location.

❧ Situate the four sidewalls on the level fort surface.

❧ Place the roof panel on top of the walls, and position it so that it covers the entire fort. Attach the roof panel by screwing one or more screws into the upright face of each 2' x 2'.

Step 5: Finish the exterior walls.

❧ Bank dirt against three exterior walls, not including the front wall with door opening. Moisten the dirt as you place it, and pack it into place.

❧ The thickness of dirt at the base should be 18 inches or more and beveled to just a few inches where the walls meet the roof.

❧ The earth walls may need repacking from time to time.

❧ Sprinkle grass seed on the outside walls and watch your fairy fort really blend in with the surroundings!

🖎 Spread white glue liberally on the door panel. Push a light layer of dry soil into the glue to make it look like a dirt wall.

Parent Tip: Go over safety rules for use of this fort including:

🖎 No playing on the roof.

🖎 Keep the door open at all times.

Fairy Fort

Construction Dates:

My Plan: Make a building plan. Take photos of the site before you build, of gathering materials, of the people who will be helping and add them here.

Construction: Tell about what happened as you built. Did things go as planned? What was fun? What was hard? Add more photos and sketches.

After Building: How have you used your new fort? What kinds of fun have you had? Write, draw, add photos and record the pleasures of having a fort!

Media Connection: Make a media journal to go along with your writing and sketches. Take photographs and create a photomontage or Keynote presentation. Record your fort building on video, and make a film of your experience using Final Cut Pro or Final Cut Express.

Post your media project on the Apple Student Gallery.

Review tutorials for Keynote, Final Cut Pro, and Final Cut Express. Tutorials can be found at www.apple.com. Select support and then the program that you are using.

10

Castle Forts

Castle Forts

Fort Focus: Castles bring forth images of queens, kings, princesses and princes. Castles often represent excitement and magic when we think of them. This activity will help you build a wonderful castle model that you can use as a guide to build a kid-size castle fort. Your finished castle fort will offer the keys to medieval times to anyone with an imagination.

Structure Story:

W*hat images come to mind when you think of castles? After you see the castle itself, do you see the royal family strolling amongst happy and peaceful subjects? Do you see a court jester entertaining the court? Is the scene grand and beautiful?*

Try this: Draw a castle scene, and show the details you see in your mind.

No matter what comes to mind, you might find the real story of castles to be very different. Throughout time, castles have mostly been used as forts! A dictionary might describe a castle as a large structure occupied by a ruler, usually a king and queen, and designed as a fort to resist attack by enemies.

Castles of the past were full of soldiers placed there for their own protection and to protect the royal family who lived separate from them. Many castles had their own kennels for keeping hunting dogs!

The first castles were wooden structures, and later stone became the main building material. It is likely that castles were mostly cold, damp places that sometimes did not smell very good since so many people lived in one place.

We think of Europe when we think of castles, but castle-like structures can be found in many parts of the world. Many homes and businesses are built to look like castles. Every now and then, you find a home with a small tower or turret to one side. Some storefronts have façades that look like the crenels, or open places, at the top of the castle that give the distinctive uneven block shape to many castles. Arched, castle-like entryways are not uncommon features in many buildings. In western Montana, there is a building supply center that looks very much like an ancient castle!

Castles conjure images that are just right for the young fort builder. Though historically they may have been places of misery and pain, as well as places of royalty and greatness, your castle offers a place of fun and imagination!

Creative thinking: Make a list of activities you would like to do in your castle fort below.

A Story Activity
Complete the story started below:

Many years ago on a windswept hill overlooking the stormy Atlantic Ocean, a young prince and princess lived lonely lives within their parent's castle. Alas, they were the only children within those castle walls, and although they had whatever they needed and their parents loved them very much, their young lives lacked excitement.

One day a rider approached the castle with a message for the king. From that moment on the young princess and prince did not need to look far for the excitement they so desired.

_____

_____

_____

_____

_____

_____

_____

_____

_____

_____

_____

_____

_____

_____

_____

_____

_____

_____

_____

_____

_____

_____

architect's model

Activity Blueprint

Fort Journal: Keep a record of your fort building experiences on the Fort Journal pages at the end of this activity. On the journal pages, you can make notes, draw sketches, and attach photographs of your fort building experience.

A Model Idea: Build your castle model on a base of plywood or sheathing material.

Castle Fort Model

Materials
• Plywood or sheathing material 1/2" or thicker, 24" x 24" or larger piece for base
• One sheet of 9" x 16" cardboard or poster board
• 1/4" plywood or hardboard: • Four 9" x 16" pieces   • Two 2 1/2" x 16" pieces   • Two 2 1/2" x 15 1/2" pieces
• Four 1" x 2" x 5" boards
• Earth-toned latex paint
• One pint of gray latex paint or one can of gray spray paint
• One black permanent marker
• Tools: Scissors, low-temperature glue gun and glue sticks, jig saw

Directions:

Step 1: Prepare the base.
◁ Paint the base with earth-toned latex paint. Let it dry as you move to the next step.

Step 2: Make a wall template.
◁ Make a template for the top edge of your castle walls out of cardboard or heavy poster board. The template should be 9" x 16".

◁ Draw lines that you can cut with scissors to create a design that looks something like the drawing.

◁ Cut out the template. Lay the template on each of the 9" x 16" pieces of plywood or hardboard. Trace carefully along the top of the template with pencil.

Step 3: Prepare the walls.

꙰ Cut out the wall tops that you outlined in pencil.

꙰ Lay the wall pieces face up on scrap boards that you have placed on newspaper outdoors. Tip: Do not lay the wall pieces directly on the newspaper because the walls will stick to the paper after you have painted them.

꙰ Using the pint of gray paint or the gray spray paint, paint one coat on each wall front. After the wall fronts have dried, paint on a second coat if needed.

꙰ When the gray paint is completely dry, use the black permanent marker to create horizontal and vertical lines on the wall fronts to make the wall look like it has uneven stones stacked beside and on top of one another.

Step 4: Assemble the walls.

꙰ When paint and marker lines are completely dry, turn the walls over. Choose one of the walls as the front of the castle.

꙰ Glue one of the 5" long 1" x 2" boards along the side of one wall and 1/4" away from the edge with the bottom edges even.

꙰ Glue another 5" long 1" x 2" board on the other side of that wall 1/4" away from the edge and with the bottoms even.

꙰ Choose a wall section for the back wall, and attach 1" x 2" x 5" boards to both sides 1/4" away from the edges as you did above.

꙰ Select one of the wall pieces without a board attached to use as a side wall and place it between the front and back wall so that it fits within the 1/4" gap. Glue it into position.

platform

🗸 Repeat with the remaining wall panel. Your walls should now be free standing.

Step 5: Attach the interior platform.
🗸 Place a good-sized squirt of glue on the top of each exposed end of the 1" x 2" board.

🗸 Quickly lay one of the 1/4" x 2 1/2" x 16" pieces flat and on top of the glue end on one side wall. Repeat with the other piece on the other side wall.

🗸 Spread glue on top and at the end of one of the pieces you just set, then lay one of the 15 1/2" pieces across the front wall and in the glue. Repeat with the other 15 1/2" piece along the back wall.

Step 6: Finish the model.
🗸 Use the black marker to draw an arched front entry gate.

🗸 You can attach the model to the base by embedding the bottom of the walls in a line of glue.

🗸 Add other details using your imagination and materials from around your yard.

Step 7: Using the model.
🗸 Use toy knights, queens, kings, and other medieval character toys as well as horses and other animals to stage battles, ceremonies, celebrations, and other events.

construction

A Child-Sized Fort

This castle fort will measure 8' x 8' with four foot walls when completed and can be taken down, moved and reassembled easily.

Parent Tip: This fort-building project requires the use of tools that require adult supervision.

Materials
• Four sheets of 3/4" x 4' x 8' exterior plywood or sheathing
• Four 2" x 2" x 4' boards
• Sixteen #12 x 2" flathead wood screws with Phillips head
• Eight 1/4" x 2 3/4" hex bolts with nuts and washers
• Two quarts semi-gloss gray exterior paint
• One pint black exterior paint
• Tools: Jig saw, adjustable wrench, pliers, power drill with 1/4" wood bit, Phillip's screwdriver

Directions:

Step 1: Find and prepare the location for your castle fort.

❧ Your fort will measure 8' x 8' when completed. Prepare a level site that is at least somewhat larger than the finished fort.

❧ If you plan to build your fort on site, make sure you have plenty of unobstructed workspace.

Step 2: Create the tops of the castle walls.

❧ On each sheet of plywood or sheathing, measure 12" down from the 8' edge, and draw a line the length of the sheet.

❧ Within that 12" space draw lines to create the uneven top of the castle wall similar to the ones you created in the model activity. Use the jigsaw to cutout the top of each wall following the lines drawn.

❧ Choose one panel to be the front wall. Draw and cut out the rounded entryway.

❧ Keep the highest point of the door at least 6" away from the previously made line at 12" from the wall top.

Step 3: Prepare the inside of the front and back wall.

ϙ Select one panel to be the back wall. Turn the panel so that the front is facing down, place it on a flat surface.

ϙ Measure in 3/4" from a 4' side and draw a line along the full 4' length. Repeat on the other side and on the other panel.

ϙ Take one of the 2" x 2" x 4' boards and position it right along the line with the 3/4" gap between it and the wall edge. Fasten the 2" x 2" x 4' board to the 3/4" panel with the #12 x 2" flathead woodscrews.

ϙ Do the same with the other three boards on the other three wall panel edges.

Parent Tip: Step 4 is a two-person step and at least one of these people need to be an adult.

Step 4: Assemble the walls.

ϙ Stand the front panel.

ϙ Stand one of the side panels next to the front panel so that the two corners fit together.

ϙ The side panel should fit into the 3/4" gap left between the 2" x 2" board and the panel edge.

ϙ Drill a 1/4" hole through the side panel corner 18" from the top so that the hole continues through the 2" x 2"

board on the front panel.

⚑ Place one of the 1/4" x 3" bolts through the hole, place a washer and nut and tighten partially.

⚑ Repeat the process with a hole 18" from the bottom.

⚑ Connect the remaining side panel, then the back panel to both sides repeating the drilling and bolting process again. Tighten all nuts.

Step 5: Finish the walls.
⚑ Paint the castle walls with one or two coats of gray exterior paint.

⚑ When this paint is dry, use the black paint to create a rough-hewn rock look by adding uneven horizontal and vertical lines as shown in the drawing on the previous page.

Step 6: Decorate your castle fort.
⚑ Add flags and other details to make your castle look realistic.

⚑ Decorate the inside to represent a particular castle room after doing further research on castles.

Step 7: Have wonderful adventures in your castle fort!

Castle Fort

Construction Dates::

My Plan: Make a building plan. Take photos of the site before you build, of gathering materials, of the people who will be helping and add them here.

Construction: Tell about what happened as you built. Did things go as planned? What was fun? What was hard? Add more photos and sketches.

After Building: How have you used your new fort? What kinds of fun have you had? Write, draw, add photos and record the pleasures of having a fort!

Media Connection: Make a media journal to go along with your writing and sketches. Take photographs and create a photomontage or Keynote presentation. Record your fort building on video, and make a film of your experience using Final Cut Pro or Final Cut Express.

Post your media project on the Apple Student Gallery.

Review tutorials for Keynote, Final Cut Pro, and Final Cut Express. Tutorials can be found at www.apple. com. Select support and then the program that you are using.